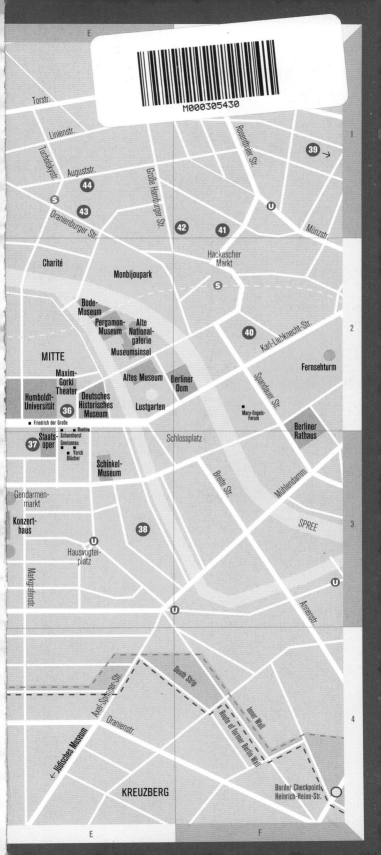

ORIENTATION Terrorized by the National Socialist dictatorship, bombarded by the Allied powers, reduced to ruins, occupied by the victors and divided for four decades by an impenetrable Wall: no other city in the world can look back on such a history. The remnants of the „Third Reich" are difficult to find in the Berlin of today, but still exist in all city districts and the surrounding countryside. The PAST FINDER® takes you to the „sights" of the past by its easy-to-use guidance system.

HOW TO USE THE PAST FINDER®
Colour-coded bars take you to the respective maps for the area specified in the bar. On the map, the numbered items in the text part are placed in the respective reference grid. The individual description of a building or site first explains its importance during the Nazi period, then its current function.

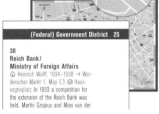

(Federal) Government District **25**

38
Reich Bank/
Ministry of Foreign Affairs
⌂ Heinrich Wolff, 1934–1938 → Werderscher Markt 1, Map E3 Ⓤ Hausvogteiplatz In 1933 a competition for the extension of the Reich Bank was held. Martin Gropius and Mies van der

LEGEND
⌂ Architect and year of construction
→ Address and grid reference on the map of the same color
Ⓢ Ⓤ Nearest S-Bahn station (urban rail system) or U-Bahn station (underground/subway system)
⊕ Opening times
▷ Reference to index

German ranks and titles are explained in the glossary on page 90.

FINDING YOUR WAY ROUND BERLIN
Berlin is one of the largest cities in Europe because of the spread of its outlying districts. When the Wall was built in 1961, two geographically and politically distinct centers developed in the ensuing decades, round the Kurfürstendamm in the West and along the street Unter den Linden in the East. This means that walking from one sight to the next may take some time. You can always use the excellent public transport system or hire a bike to explore the capital.

Tourist Information
→ Brandenburg Gate, Southern Wing
⊕ Mon–Sat 9.30–18.00
→ Budapester Straße, Europa Center
⊕ Mon–Sun 8.00–22.00
→ Television Tower, Panoramastraße
⊕ Mon–Sun 9.30–18.00
→ Tegel Airport, Haupthalle/Main Hall
⊕ Mon–Sun 5.00–22.30

Berlin Transport Authority (Berliner Verkehrsgesellschaft/BVG)
Information on subway (U-Bahn), city train (S-Bahn), tram and bus routes and times are available at every station or stop. Timetables, issued free of charge, and information can be obtained at all regional and long-distance train stations. Tickets can be bought at ticket machines on all platforms or at the counters.

Bikes for Hire from the Deutsche Bahn (DB/German Railroad)
This is what you do: find a bike painted silver and red with a DB logo, phone the number stated, pay by credit card, enter PIN and pedal off.

Velo Taxi
Simply flag down one of the streamlined rikshas, climb in and enjoy the ride.

PAST FINDER BERLIN

CH. LINKS VERLAG, BERLIN

36 Göring, Hitler and Hindenburg on the Heroes' Memorial Day 1934 in front of the „Neue Wache" on Unter den Linden

(FEDERAL) GOVERNMENT DISTRICT It is difficult to imagine how busy life used to be in this part of Berlin. Here, the Second World War and the division into East and West Berlin have left the biggest scars in the cityscape. Along Wilhelmstraße was the seat of power of the „Third Reich". From here, Hitler and his henchmen terrorized the whole of Europe. Only a few buildings and numerous bunkers have survived. One of the few exhibitions in the center of Berlin telling the story of the National Socialist regime is the „Topography of Terror" in the foundations of the former Gestapo headquarters.

1
Brandenburg Gate

⌂ Carl Gotthard Langhans, 1791 → Pariser Platz, Map C2 Ⓢ Unter den Linden The Brandenburg Gate is the ultimate symbol of German history. The statue on top, the goddess of peace with her chariot and four horses, designed by Johann Gottfried Schadow, was taken to Paris in 1806, on Napoleon's order, and was returned in 1815 after Napoleon's defeat at Waterloo. An iron cross, forged from „blood and iron", and the Prussian eagle was added to the wreath, making the statue the goddess of victory. When Hitler came to power in January 1933, SA troops marched through the Gate. Parades were held in 1937 for Benito Mussolini, in 1939 for Hitlers 50th birthday, and in 1940 the Wehrmacht celebrated their victory in the Blitzkrieg against Poland and France. Five years later, the Allied forces paraded at the end of the Second World War here among the ruins of Berlin. In 1961 the Brandenburg Gate became part of the „Todesstreifen", the death strip along the Berlin Wall and was only returned to public access on 22 December 1989.

2
Central Office of the Inspector General for Road Construction / Central Office of the Reich Minister for Armaments and War Production / DZ Bank

⌂ Frank O. Gehry, 1999 → Pariser Platz 3, Map C3 Ⓢ Unter den Linden As early as 1933 the engineer Fritz Todt was made Inspector General for Road

Construction by Hitler. He was to prove his organizational talents by building the Reichsautobahn (Highways). In 1938 the ▷ „Organisation Todt" was formed to build the West Wall (fortifications along the German-French border). With its over one million laborers it was also responsible for the erection of bunkers and fortifications. In March 1940 Todt was made Minister for Armaments and Munitions. After the failed attempt to capture Moscow in December 1941, Todt repeatedly urged Hitler to end a war that could not be won. Hitler refused. On 8 February 1942, Todt died in a plane crash, the cause of which was never fully established. His grave is in the ▷ **Invaliden Cemetery**. The Ministry Building was destroyed in the war; the new building with its spectacular interior was designed by the Californian avant-garde architect Frank O. Gehry in 1999.

3
Central Office of the Inspector General for Construction in the Reich Capital Berlin / Academy of Fine Arts

⌂ Behnisch & Partner, 2005 → Pariser Platz 2, Map C3 Ⓢ Unter den Linden On Hitler's orders, Albert Speer was made Inspector General for Building Construction in the „Reich" Capital Berlin and moved into the building of the former Academy of Fine Arts in 1937. From the ▷ **Old Chancellery**, via the Ministry Gardens, Hitler now had easy access to the studios which have survived to this day. In the following years, he came almost daily to discuss with Speer their plans for a monumental reconstruction

TIME LINE OF GERMAN HISTORY 1914–1990

1914 Beginning of First World War

1918 End of First World War
November Revolution in Berlin
Kaiser Wilhelm II resigns

1929 World Economic Crisis

30 January 1933
Hitler appointed
Reich Chancellor

1 August 1936
XI Olympic Games

1 September 1939
Invasion of Poland,
Start of Second
World War

1941 Invasion
the Soviet Unic

19-

Empire	Weimar Republic	"Third Reich"
	1918	1933

of Berlin as the new metropolis „Germania", poring over a 30 m long model, often well into the night. Speer took over the responsibilities of the deceased Fritz Todt in February 1942, also claiming the neighboring building of the ▷ **Inspectorate for Road Management**. In 1943, Speer's ministerial duties were subsumed under the new title of Minister of Armaments and War Production. After the war, up to 1950, the Academy of Arts of the GDR was situated in the severely damaged building. In 2005, a new building, constructed around the core of the old one, was opened as the new seat of the Academy of Fine Arts.

4
Hotel Adlon

⌂ Patzschke, Klotz & Partner, 1997 → Unter den Linden 75–77, Map C3 Ⓢ Unter den Linden Before the war, the hotel was a legend among the luxury hotels of the world. If you could afford it, this was the place to stay in Berlin. Because of the bombing raids on Berlin, a luxury bunker was constructed underneath the hotel in the 1940s. During the Battle of Berlin the hotel was used as a hospital and severely damaged. The ruins were demolished after the war, and the new hotel was opened in 1997.

5
Max Liebermann's House

⌂ Friedrich August Stüler, 1846 → Pariser Platz 7, Map C2 Ⓢ Unter den Linden „**I can't eat as much as I'd like to throw up,**" is the legendary remark made by the Jewish painter Max Liebermann, after watching SA troops march through the ▷ **Brandenburg Gate** hour after hour, to celebrate Hitler's appointment as Reich Chancellor on

30 January 1933. Liebermann's paintings were later banned. His death in 1935 saved the former director of the ▷ **Academy of Fine Arts** from imprisonment in a concentration camp. Facing deportation to Theresienstadt concentration camp, his wife committed suicide in 1943. Liebermann's summer villa (Am Großen Wannsee 42), forcibly sold in 1940, today houses a public museum. His estate on Pariser Platz today is the headquarters of a cultural foundation.

6
Reichstag

⌂ Paul Wallot, 1894; Sir Norman Foster, 1999 → Platz der Republik 1, Map C2 Ⓢ Unter den Linden ⏲ Mon–Sun 8–22 After the foundation of the German Reich in 1871, the Reichstag was designed as a representative building for the parliament. Building work started in 1884 and the inauguration was on 5 December 1894. The Kaiser, who disliked the architect and parliamentarism equally, called the building the „**height of bad taste**". It took nearly 20 years for Kaiser Wilhelm II to agree to the inscription of the words „**Dem Deutschen Volke**" (To the German People) being put in place on the façade during the First World War. „Pure satire," commented writer Kurt Tucholsky. The Kaiser provided two French canons,

	13 August 1961	
	Erection of Berlin Wall	
ttle of Stalingrad		
May 1945	**23 May 1949** Foundation of the Federal Republic of Germany (FRG)	**9 November 1989**
nd of Second	**7 October 1949** Foundation of the German Democratic Republic (GDR)	Fall of Berlin Wall
orld War		GDR joins FRG on
	17 June 1953 People's Uprising in Berlin and the GDR	3 October 1990
1948 Soviet Blockade of Berlin		

FRG / GDR	**Germany**
	1989

captured in the Wars of Liberation in 1813, to cast the letters, which were designed by famous architect Peter Behrens. After the burning of the Reichstag on 28 February 1933, details of which are still unclear to this day, the building remained unused. Yet for the Red Army it was the most important symbol of Nazi Germany. At dawn on the 30 April 1945, Soviet soldiers attacked the building, which was defended by what remained of the French Waffen-SS division „Charlemagne" who had turned the building into a fortress. It wasn't until the evening that the Soviet soldiers managed to penetrate into the interior of the building.

Finally, at midnight Moscow time, the red flag was flown from the roof. While the end of the war was being celebrated around the Brandenburg Gate, the defendants kept up their fight in the cellars, sometimes with only knives and spades, until the following midday of the 2 May 1945, when Soviet troops put an end to the fighting by using flame-throwers. On 9 September 1948, 300 000 Berliners assembled on Platz der Republik to demonstrate against the Soviet blockade of Berlin. The glass dome, destroyed in the war, was reconstructed in modern style by Norman Foster and is accessible to the public. Today, the historic building is one of the most prominent symbols of German reunification.

In 1999, the Reichstag once again became the seat of the German parliament.

7
Soviet War Memorial
⌂ Kerbel, Zigal, Sergiyevski, 1945
→ Straße des 17. Juni, Map B2
Ⓢ Unter den Linden The first Soviet war memorial in Berlin was erected on 11 November 1945, precisely at the point where the north-south and east-west axes were to meet according to Speer's plans for the new Berlin. Two Soviet T34 tanks flank a colonnade on which stands a Red Army soldier; granite slabs from the ▷ **New Reich Chancellery** were used for the construction. In the park behind are buried 2 200 soldiers who lost their lives storming the ▷ **Reichstag**. Underneath, three motorway tunnels from 60 to 220 meters long, dating from the Nazi time, were discovered in 1967. They were to be part of a junction-free system of tunnels under the axes' intersection point. Towards the end of the war, armament companies set up production here, protected from the bombs, and thousands of people found shelter from the air raids.

8
Kroll Opera House
⌂ Langhans, Persicus, Knoblauch, 1844 → Entlastungsstraße, Map B2
Ⓢ Unter den Linden After the ▷ **Reichstag's** burning in 1933, the Kroll Opera House, across from the Reichstag, was used for „par-liamentary" sessions during the „Third Reich". Under the swastika emblem, German parliamentary history reached its nadir with the passing of the „Enabling Law" on 24 March

Adolf Hitler 1889–1945

Adolf Hitler was born on 20 April 1989, the son of customs official Alois Hitler and his wife Clara in Braunau on the Inn in Austria. After the death of his parents he left for Vienna in 1907, without ever finishing his secondary education. He twice failed to secure entry into the Academy of Fine Arts, supported himself from a small allowance, and painted sketches for sale. Anti-Semitic literature increasingly formed his outlook on life; he developed a hatred of Marxism, liberalism and Jewish people. At the start of the First World War he volunteered for the 16th Bavarian Reserve Infantry Regiment. Private first class Hitler received the Iron Cross, Second and First Class, later was blinded temporarily by poison gas. Hitler saw the German capitulation in 1918 as a **„stab in the army's back by the Jews and Communists"** and decided to devote himself to politics. In 1919, in a letter, he describes the **complete removal of the Jews** as his most pressing political goal. He worked as a spy for the German army and joined the „German Workers' Party", one of the many right-wing splinter groups, as part of his job as an informer. The party renamed itself „National Socialist German Workers' Party" (NSDAP) in 1920. After the abortive Munich putsch in 1923, he was sentenced to five years imprisonment for treason, but released after only nine months. It was during his imprisonment that he started writing **„Mein Kampf"** (My Struggle), his personal political manifesto. With a steady increase in electoral strength, the NSDAP became the second largest party in Parliament by 1932, and on 30 January 1933 Hitler was offered the chancellorship by the conservative parties in parliament. As early as 1933 he had persuaded the German military to his political mission, and in 1941, with the invasion of the Soviet Union, he felt himself close to his final goals. In 1942, at the maximum height of his power, German troops occupied a territory reaching from Africa to the North Cape, from the Atlantic to the oilfields of the Caucasus. But Hitler had not learned his lesson from Napoleon's fate: soon thereafter success began to elude him and the war finally returned to its place of origin. On 29 April 1945 Hitler appointed Grand Admiral Dönitz his successor. In the ▷**„Führer Bunker"** people tried to persuade Hitler to flee, but in vain. On 30 April, around 3.30 p.m., Hitler committed suicide, together with his girlfriend Eva Braun, whom he had married only hours before.

„Obeying orders is enough up to the level of general, then responsibility begins." (Frederick the Great)

Adolf Hitler visits conquered Paris in June 1940, here at the Trocadéro. To his right are architect Albert Speer and sculptor Arno Breker, to his left architect Hermann Giesler.

1933. From now on, Hitler had the power to pass laws without the consent of either Parliament or Reich President. Six years later, on 1 September 1939, Hitler announced the invasion of Poland

make space for the ▷ **Great Hall**. The Soviets used it as a command center during the storming of the ▷ **Reichstag**; in 1992 it again became the Embassy of the Swiss Confederation.

6 Soviet graffiti

6 Reichstag Building

6 American graffiti

by German troops from here, giving the following (false) reasons:
„Tonight for the first time Polish regular soldiers have fired on our territory. Since 5.45 a.m. we have been returning the fire, and from now on bombs will be met by bombs. ... One word I have never learned: that is, surrender."
On 22 September 1943, the opera house was destroyed during an air raid. Today, in its place, there is a park.

9
Embassy of the Swiss Confederation
⌂ Friedrich Hitzig, 1870 → Otto-von-Bismarck-Allee 4, Map B2 ⓢ Hauptbahnhof/Lehrter Bahnhof The fact that Hitler saw the German Swiss population as „millions of German nationals", increasingly worried the neutral Switzerland, by 1940 encircled on all sides by the „Axis" powers. The Swiss ambassador to Berlin, Hans Frölicher, advised his government to join Hitler's „New Europe". Nothing of the kind happened, but gold deposits by the German ▷ **Reichsbank** were welcome in Swiss safes and provided new funds for the „Third Reich" enabling it to continue the war. That the gold was taken from those who had died in concentration camps or had been stolen from the occupied territories was not an issue. In 1955 Switzerland began trying to find the real owners and to return the so-called „Nazi gold" to the victims' relatives.
The embassy building is the only one to survive the air raids as well as the Nazis' demolition policy in the area to

10
Wilhelm Street
→ Wilhelmstraße, Map C3 ⓤ Mohrenstraße From the beginning of the 19th century, the Wilhelmstraße, named after King Friedrich Wilhelm I of Prussia, was the proverbial heart of the government district. Prussia's most important ministries were situated here, those of the German Reich, the embassies of the European superpowers, and, from 1933, the center of the Nazi regime. Adolf Hitler, Albert Speer, Hermann Göring, Joseph Goebbels, Rudolf Hess, Heinrich Himmler, Reinhard Heydrich – they all had their offices here. Nearly all the buildings were damaged in the final Battle of Berlin and razed to the ground after the war.
For four decades leaves of grass covered the soil where some of the most gruesome crimes of human history had been planned. The Wall only a few meters away, this area was next to the „death strip" (security zone on the eastern side of the Wall).
In the 1980s Plattenbauten (apartment blocks) were put up by the GDR-government, making the former administrative district a residential area. Nearby Wilhelmplatz lost all traces of its 250-year long architectural history. On the grounds of the adjacent former hotel „Kaiserhof", North Korea built its embassy, Czechoslovakia erected a concrete and glass embassy building next door. Today, only a few restored prewar buildings, used by Federal Government ministries, remain in the Wilhelmstraße as reminders of the old government district.

The Center of Power

11
Central Office of the „Führer's" Deputy/Federal Ministry of Consumer Protection, Nutrition and Agriculture

⌂ Carl Vohl 1903 → Wilhelmstraße 54, Map C3 Ⓤ Mohrenstraße This building used to be the liaison office of the King of Prussia and Kaiser of Germany to the respective government. After Hitler came to power, the NSDAP made it Ribben-

press, radio, publishing, art, theaters and film were supervised by the Ministry and forced to conform to Nazi laws and decrees. The ministry was given the Building of the former governmental press office, originally built in the early 18th century. To house the growing number of employees an extension was built towards the rear of the building, which is still standing today, while the old building was destroyed

12 Ministry of Propaganda

13 Old Chancellery, 1930

11 Hess' Former Central Office

trop's office and the party's liaison office, both under the command of the „Führer's" deputy, Rudolf Hess. His job was to make sure that all directives, laws and party promotions conformed to the Nazi ideology. After Hess' flight to Great Britain in 1941, Martin Bormann was made his successor.

In the Nuremberg military tribunal, Hess was sentenced to life imprisonment and committed suicide in ▷ Spandau prison in 1987. Bormann's body was found during construction excavations at Lehrter Station in 1972; after fleeing from the ▷ „Führer Bunker" he had committed suicide here together with Hitler's personal physician Ludwig Stumpfegger on 2 May 1945.

12
Ministry of Public Enlightenment and Propaganda/Federal Ministry of Health and Social Security

⌂ 1737; Karl Reichle, 1936 → Wilhelmstraße 49/Mauerstraße 45–53, Map D3 Ⓤ Mohrenstraße On 13 March 1933 the Reich Ministry of Public Enlightenment and Propaganda was founded and the Gauleiter (regional leader) of the NSDAP in Berlin, Joseph Goebbels, was put in charge. All cultural institutions,

during allied airraids in 1945. After removal of all Nazi emblems, the remaining part of the building was used as the office of the „National Council of the National Front" of the GDR. Today, it is the home of the Federal Ministry of Health and Social Security.

13
Old Chancellery

⌂ C.F. Richter, 1734; E.J. Siedler, 1928 → Wilhelmstraße 77, Map C3 Ⓤ Mohrenstraße „No power in the world will ever get me out of here alive," Hitler is reported to have said, when he moved in in 1933, after his election as Reich Chancellor. The building had been the Chancellery of the German Reich since 1878. Otto von Bismarck and Friedrich Ebert resided here.

From 1934 to 1939, the building housed Hitler's office and private apartment. Hitler added a hall and an air-raid shelter underneath. The latter was extended in 1944 and became the famous ▷ „Führer Bunker". The remains of the building were razed to the ground in 1949. Today, the street „An der Kolonnade" passes through the grounds. Only a few plaques remind us that here was once the seat of political power in Germany.

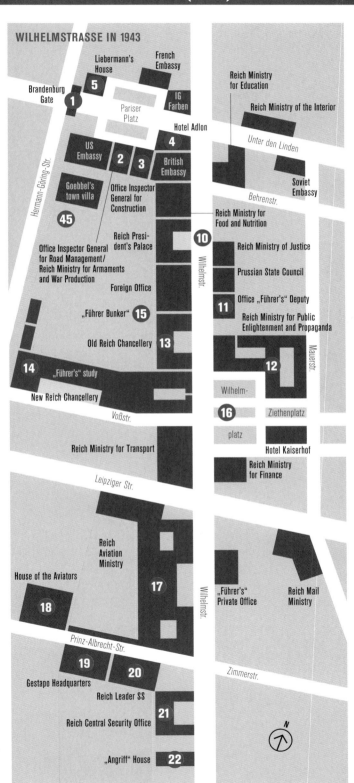

14 New Chancellery, Voßstraße

14 „Leibstandarte" (personal guard) at the entrance

14 Court of Honour with Statues by Breker

14 Hitler's study

14 Marble Gallery

15 Excavated foundations of the New Chancellery

The New Reich Chancellery

14

New Reich Chancellery

⌂ Albert Speer, 1936–1939 → Voß-straße 2–6, Map C3 Ⓤ Mohrenstraße

In 1935 Hitler's favourite architect Albert Speer was commissioned to build a new Chancellery, and after 3 years of construction the building was inaugurated in January 1939. The new Chancellery was to reflect Germany's increase in power and importance, according to Nazi propaganda. The ground plan of the 421 m long building was designed to impress or intimidate and mark the „Führer's" distance from ordinary mortals. Visitors had to traverse a flight of rooms 300 meters long, the so-called „Diplomats' Promenade", including a marble gallery, at 146 meters double the size of the Gallery of Mirrors in Versailles. Hitler's office was clad in marble and of gigantic proportions with its nearly 400 square meters and a height of 10 meters. The „Court of Honour" with statues by sculptor Arno Breker, a greenhouse and two houses for Hitlers Bodyguards, the Reichssicherheitsdienst (Reich Security Service) completed the building complex. After the war, none of the ruined government buildings were to be left as reminders of the Nazi regime. On 13 October 1948, an order was given by the Soviet Administration for Berlin to raze all buildings in Voss Straße and on Wilhelmplatz to the ground. The granite blocks and the marble of the New Chancellery were used for the construction of ▷ **Soviet war memorials** and the decoration of the underground station ▷ **„Mohrenstraße"**.

15

„Führer Bunker"

⌂ Carl Piepenburg, 1944 → Voß-straße 4–6, Map C3 Ⓤ Mohrenstraße

In 1935 an air-raid shelter for 150 people was built underneath the hall of the ▷ **Old Chancellery**. This was transformed into an „ante-bunker" in 1944, while adjacent the actual „Führer Bunker" was constructed, for 1.4 million Reichmarks. It was 12 meters below ground level, side walls and ceiling were 4 meters thick. This last command center of the „Third Reich" was built as working and living quarters for Hitler and his immediate personal staff. The **„Führer's" escort guard** with 250 men under the command of SS Major General Johann Rattenhuber was responsible for Hitler's personal protection. The very last days in the cramped and dank rooms were spent in an atmosphere of imminent doom. Faced with the prospect of inevitable defeat, Hitler prepared for his death on 30 April 1945. He asked his closest staff to make sure to burn his corpse, as he did not want to fall into the hands of the Red Army, neither dead nor alive, to be exhibited as a „war trophy" in Moscow. Around 15.30 Hitler committed suicide together with Eva Braun, whom he had married shortly before. In the garden of the Reich Chancellery the corpses were dowsed in petrol and then burnt. Some teeth and a few bones were all that remained of Hitler's body. On the 1 May, after killing their six children, Goebbels and his wife shot themselves. Their burnt bodies were displayed by the Soviets as

„The Party": larger-than-life statue by Arno Breker for the Court of Honour at the New Reich Chancellery

„Führer Bunker"

„FÜHRER BUNKER"

1 Adolf Hitler's sleeping quarters
2 Adolf Hitler's living quarters
3 Adolf Hitler's and Eva Braun's bathroom and dressing room
4 Toilets and washrooms
5 Eva Braun's sleeping and living quarters
6 Adolf Hitler's study
7 Situation and conference room
8 Waiting room for conference participants
9 Ante-room and hall
10 Generators and ventilation system
11 Martin Bormann's study
12 Joseph Goebbels' study
13 Joseph Goebbels' sleeping quarters
14 Ludwig Stumpfegger's sleeping quarters
15 Ludwig Stumpfegger's surgery
16 Telephone exchange and telegraph office
17 Outside exhaust ventilator
18 Day room for members of Reich Security Service and „Führer" escort guard, „dog bunker" and access outside exhaust ventilator
19 Reich Security-Service
20 Gas lock
21 Exit to Reich Chancellery Garden
22 Reich Security Service, gas lock and stairs up to ante-bunker on upper floor

Hitler's and Eva Braun's bodies were placed in a shell crater, close to the exit of the „Führer Bunker", doused in about 10 canisters of petrol and burned by Hitler's adjutant Otto Günsche and valet Heinz Linge

ANTE-BUNKER
23 Old gas lock
24 Ante-room
25 Living and sleeping quarters for
    Magda Goebbels and Children
26 Servants' sleeping quarters
27 Day room Reich
    Security Service
28 Generators and ventilation system
29 Canteen
30 Toilets and washrooms
31 Kitchen for Hitler's dietician
    Constanze Manziarly
32 Store room
33 Day room
34 Safe
35 Sleeping quarters
36 Reich Security Service
37 Gas locks
38 Emergency exit to garden
    of Foreign Ministry
39 Main entrance and tunnel to bunker
    system of the New Reich Chancellery

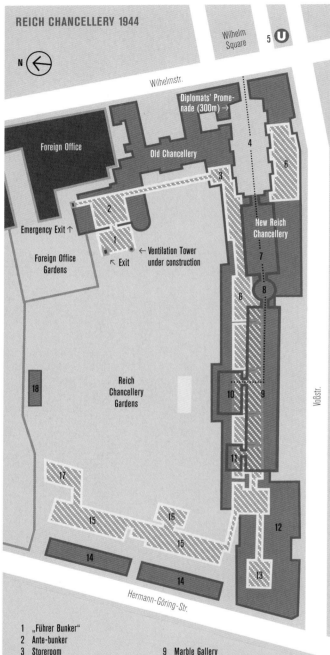

REICH CHANCELLERY 1944

Wilhelm Square

5 Ⓤ

N

Wilhelmstr.

Diplomats' Promenade (300m) →

Foreign Office

Old Chancellery

4

6

3

2

New Reich Chancellery

Emergency Exit ↑

1

← Ventilation Tower under construction

7

↖ Exit

Foreign Office Gardens

6

8

Reich Chancellery Gardens

18

10

9

Voßstr.

11

17

16

12

15

15

13

14

14

Hermann-Göring-Str.

1   „Führer Bunker"
2   Ante-bunker
3   Storeroom
4   Court of Honour
5   Subway Station „Kaiserhof"
     (today: „Mohrenstraße")
6   Military hospital and bunker
     for Bormann, Krebs, Burgdorf,
     Hitler's pilot Baur, adjutants,
     radio operator etc.
7   Mosaics Hall
8   Round Hall

9   Marble Gallery
10   Hitler's study
11   Reich Cabinet meeting room
12   Administrative wing
13   Car park bunker
14   Residential building of the Reich Security Service
15   Underground car park
16   Driver's bunker (preserved)
17   Garage bunker
18   Greenhouse

a proof of their death. First attempts to demolish the ante-bunker were made by the Soviets in 1947.

As part of the GDR building plans for the site in 1988, the ceiling of the main bunker was laboriously demolished. The base plate and parts of the wall are still there.

Completely destroyed in the war, the underground station was reopened in 1950 under the name „Thälmannplatz". The red marble from the „Mosaics Hall" in the ▷ New Reich Chancellery was used in its construction. Today, the subway station is called „Mohren-straße".

15 Driver's shelter, 1990

14 Hitler's marble in the Mosaics Hall ...

16 ... and today underground

In 1990 the drivers' bunker for Hitler's fleet of cars was found, 8 by 30 meters, on Ebertstraße, with eight murals with SS themes.

Afraid that this somber location might become a shrine for neo-Nazis, the city council of Berlin decided to seal up the rooms.

16
Subway Station „Kaiserhof" / Subway Station „Mohrenstraße"

⌂ Alfred Grenander, 1950 → Mohren-straße, Map D3 Ⓤ Mohrenstraße

The subway station was originally called „Kaiserhof", after the hotel on adjacent Wilhelmsplatz, where Hitler and Goebbels often met since September 1930.

In the last hours of the war, on 1 May 1945, shortly before midnight, about ten groups escaped from the ▷ „Führer Bunker" via the subway tunnel towards „Friedrichstraße" station. Wilhelm Mohnke, SS major general in charge of the defense sector „**Citadel**", was the instigator of the break-out attempt and led the first group with SS-Hauptsturm-führer Otto Günsche and Hitler's secre-taries.

Other groups followed, among them Johann Rattenhuber, Martin Bormann, Hitler's chief pilot Hans Baur, his chauf-feur Erich Kempka, his valet Heinz Linge and about a hundred people living in the bunker. Only a few managed to escape to Northern Germany, as planned. Many died in the house-to-house fighting or were captured by the Soviets.

17
Reich Aviation Ministry / Federal Ministry of Finance

⌂ Ernst Sagebiel, 1935 – 1936
→ Wilhelmstraße 97, Map C4
Ⓢ Ⓤ Potsdamer Platz

The building of the Reich Aviation Ministry was one of the first major construction projects of the Nazis in Berlin. The rearmament of the German Armed Forces was in 1935 in full swing, and Göring's favourite goal was to establish a new German Airforce. The building was to house the administration of the Airforce.

When the building was finished after a construction period of only two years, it was, with its 2 000 rooms, the largest building in Berlin.

In keeping with its function, the bani-ster was made from aircraft aluminum and the lighting in the Leipziger Straße foyer was modeled on anti-aircraft gun searchlights.

From the spacious hall Hermann Göring commanded the German air force and promised the German people if ever an enemy airplane entered German air-space, they could call him Meyer (i.e. „John Doe").

The ministry was hit by a bomb only once, while the surrounding buildings were more or less completely destroyed. During GDR times, several ministries were housed here. Today the building has been restored to its original state and houses the Federal Ministry of Finance.

18
„House of the Aviators"/ Berlin State Parliament

⌂ Friedrich Schulze, 1892 → Niederkirchnerstraße 5, Map C4 Ⓢ Ⓤ Potsdamer Platz Here, until Hitler's appointment as chancellor, was the seat of the Prussian Parliament, which was abolished on 18 May 1933. In 1939 Hermann Göring had the building converted to the „House of the Aviators", an air force officers' club, and connected to the adjacent ▷ Air Force Ministry. Since 1993 the building houses the Berlin State Parliament.

Right: Badge of the Prussian criminal police force

19
„Gestapo" Headquarters/„Topography of Terror"

⌂ 1905 → Niederkirchnerstraße 8, Map C4 Ⓢ Ⓤ Potsdamer Platz Here, in 1933, Hermann Göring set up the headquarters of the Secret State Police (**Ge**heime **Sta**ats**po**lizei – „Gestapo"). Under the command of Heinrich Himmler and Reinhard Heydrich the ▷ „Gestapo" developed into an instrument of terror against political opponents and the Jewish population. The building was destroyed in the war, and in the remains of the cellar and the cell floors of the infamous „house prison", the ▷ „Topography of Terror" exhibition is installed. A comprehensive Nazi documentation center is planned.

20
Central Office of the „Reichsführer SS"/„Topography of Terror"

⌂ Wesenberg, 1788 → Niederkirchnerstraße 9, Map D4 Ⓢ Ⓤ Potsdamer Platz Built as Hotel „Vier Jahreszeiten" (Four Seasons), later renamed Hotel „Prinz Albrecht", the building was used from an early stage as a meeting place by Hitler and Goebbels. In 1934 the former hotel became Heinrich Himmler's office as „Reichsführer SS", the streetname „Prinz Albrecht Straße" became the synonym for Nazi terror in Berlin.

From his desk Himmler planned and ruthlessly instigated the creation of an Aryan, racially-pure Germany, the conquest of Lebensraum (national living area) and a national-political reorganization of Europe. The ruins of the building were razed to the ground after the war.

21
Reich Central Security Office/„Topography of Terror"

⌂ Karl-Friedrich Schinkel, 1833 → Wilhelmstraße 102, Map D4 Ⓢ Ⓤ Potsdamer Platz From 1934, the „Prinz Albrecht Palais" was Reinhard Heydrich's office as head of the Nazi Security Service (**S**icherheits**d**ienst – SD). In 1939 Heinrich Himmler made him also responsible for the Reich Security Central Office (**R**eich**ss**icherheits**h**aupt**a**mt – RSHA), which combined nearly all the security departments of the „Third Reich". The ruins of the building were razed to the ground after the war.

22
„Angriff" House/„Topography of Terror"

→ Wilhelmstraße 106, Map D4 Ⓢ Ⓤ Potsdamer Platz In 1932, the Nazi newspaper **„Der Angriff"** (The Attack), founded in 1927 by Joseph Goebbels as a NSDAP propaganda instrument for Berlin, moved from Hedemannstraße 10 (regional headquarters of the NSDAP) to Wilhelmstraße. Goebbels used the newspaper to discredit and persecute the political opponents of the Nazis. From 1934, the **„Angriff"** was resident in Zimmerstraße 68–91. The last issue with 300 000 copies was published on 24 April 1945. After the „Angriff" had moved out in 1934, this building was used briefly by the SA, then by the SS. The entry to the former courtyard, still visible in the pavement, and a plaque of the „Topography of Terror" exhibition are the last traces of the building, which was destroyed during the war.

„Topography of Terror"

The „Prinz Albrecht Straße" district, between 1933 and 1945, was the command center from which the National Socialist regime organized and spread its terror over the whole of Europe. Here, combined in the ▷ **Reich Central Security Office** (RSHA),

sination attempt by Czech freedom fighters and died soon after. The Nazi regime mourned the death of this man who had proven his talent for terror and whom many had considered a suitable successor to Hitler.

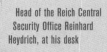

20 Exhibition area

were the Gestapo headquarters, the ▷ **Central Office of the Reichsführer SS**, Heinrich Himmler, and the Central Office of the chief of the Security Police and the Security Service (SD), Reinhard Heydrich. At this historic site, the „Topography of Terror" exhibition provides information about persecution and murder of people all over Europe.

Reinhard Heydrich 1904–1942

Heydrich, a rabid anti-Semite, was one of the key figures in the ruthless expulsion and extermination of the European Jews. As head of the Reich Central Security Office, the executive was combined in his hand: Criminal Investigation Department, Security Service and Gestapo. He was the master of life and death. After a failed career in the navy, young Heydrich applied to Himmler, who was putting together a „SS"-secret service. The duo formed a fatal combination of racist cleansing mania and ice-cold sense of power. Following the German assault of the Soviet Union, their Einsatzgruppen killed hundreds of thousands behind the front. Armed with a letter of authority for the implementation of the „**final solution to the Jewish question**", Heydrich planned the killing of 11 million European Jews. On 27 May 1942, Heydrich was injured in an assas-

The Gestapo

Since April 1933, all German federal states had a Secret State Police Force (**Ge**heime **Sta**ats**po**lizei – Gestapo), created by Hermann Göring. Under Heydrich, the Gestapo developed into a national political police force, which systematically persecuted all political opponents of the Nazi regime. Those considered „work-shy" or „antisocial", but above all „communists" and „social-democrats", were taken into „**protective custody**", tortured, imprisoned in concentration camps, or killed right away. Fear of being reported to the Gestapo by one's neighbour was all-pervasive.

Star of David

According to a police directive of 1 September 1941, the yellow „Star of David" („Judenstern" or Jewish star) **had to be worn, sewn on the left side of the chest**, well visible. The Nazi regime thus took up the medieval practice of stigmatizing Jews.

Head of the Reich Central Security Office Reinhard Heydrich, at his desk

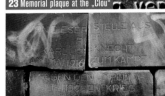

23 Memorial plaque at the „Clou"

26 Liebknecht-Memorial in the courtyard of the Lapidarium

17 Court of Honour of the Reich Aviation Ministry

26 Statues from the Siegesallee at the Lapidarium

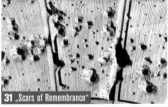

31 „Scars of Remembrance"

20 „Topography of Terror" with Berlin Wall

17 Mural from GDR times

23
Clou Ballroom and Concert Hall
⌂ Hermann Blankenstein, 1886
→ Zimmerstraße 68 – 91, Map D4
Ⓤ Kochstraße The ballroom was used
as a meeting hall by the Nazis. On 1 May
1927 Hitler appeared here in Berlin
for a first Nazi mass event. In the
ante-house and the annex the propaganda papers **„Völkischer Beobachter"**,
„Schwarzes Korps", and **„Der Angriff"**
were printed. The Gestapo used the cellar for interrogations and torture. During
the **SS-„Operation Factory"**, the ballroom
served as the assembly camp for hundreds of Jewish forced laborers in 1943.
After the war, the building, now situated
next to the Berlin Wall, was a no-go
area, and used by the GDR soldiers as
an office and a place to warm up.

24
„Organisation Todt"/ Employment Center of Berlin and Brandenburg
⌂ Hans Fritzsche, 1941 → Friedrich-
straße 34 – 37a, Map D4 Ⓤ Kochstraße
Lacking the necessary building materials, which were needed to build the
West Wall (rampart along the German-
French border), this building, planned
as the regional employment office,
remained a shell until 1939. In his po-
sition as Minister for Armaments and
Munitions, Fritz Todt offered to finish
the building, if allowed to use it for his
own organization, which took seat here.
Albert Speer was appointed his successor after Todt's fatal plane crash in
February 1942 and took also over the
„Organisation Todt". A monumental Reich
eagle remains on the middle projection
of the building.

25
Anhalter Railway Station and Shelter
⌂ Franz Schwechten, 1880 → Askani-
scher Platz 6 – 7, Map C4 Ⓢ Anhalter
Bahnhof ⏱ Mon, Tue, Thu, Sun 10 – 19,
Fri 10 – 20, Sat 12 – 20
The hall of Europe's once largest termi-
nus station was originally 170 meters
long, 62 meters wide, with a height of

34 meters and a ceiling made of glass
and steel. On 3 February 1945, a heavy
air raid destroyed most of the building.
Only six months after the war, parts
of the station were operational again.
In spite of massive public protests, the
parts of the building above ground were
demolished in 1959. A fragment of the
entrance portal remains as a memorial.
The neighboring bunker in Schöneberger
Straße provided shelter for the railway
personnel and up to 12 000 civilians.
There is an exhibition of the history of
the bunker, and next to it, a „Chamber
of Horrors".

26
Pumping Station / Lapidarium
⌂ James Hobrecht, 1873 → Hallesches
Ufer 78, Map C4 Ⓤ Mendelssohn-
Bartholdy-Park ⏱ Mon – Thu, Sat – Sun
10 – 18 Here, in the disused pumping
station, the sculptures of the former
Prussian Siegesallee (Avenue of Victo-
ries) in Tiergarten are being stored. The
Allied powers removed the statues and
buried them next to Schloss Bellevue.
Today, here in the Lapidarium, you can
visit Otto the Lazy, Heinrich the Child,
Frederick the Great and other stony-
faced dignitaries.

27
Apartment Mies van der Rohe
→ Am Karlsbad 24, Map B4 Ⓢ Ⓤ Potsdamer Platz Ludwig Mies van der Rohe
came to Berlin in 1905 to study architecture, and lived in this distinguished
apartment house. In the 1920s he got
famous for designing the plans for a
glass skyscraper in Friedrichstraße and
was commissioned to build a residential
complex in Afrikanische Straße 15 – 41.
The ▷ **Bauhaus Berlin**, managed by Mies,
was dissolved by the Nazis in 1933,
and in 1937 Mies emigrated to Chicago.
He designed the Neue Nationalgalerie,
opened in 1968. The founder of the
Bauhaus, Walter Gropius, designed the
Bauhaus Archive in 1964, originally
meant to be situated in Darmstadt, but
built in Klingelhöferstraße 14. Exhibits
on Bauhaus history and changing exhibitions can be viewed there.

German Resistance Movement

Claus von Stauffenberg
1907–1944

As an officer in a Panzer division, Stauffenberg took part in the wars against Poland and France in 1939 and 1940. Shocked by the massmurders following the German assault of the Soviet Union, he joined the military resistance group around Colonel-General Ludwig Beck and General Friedrich Olbricht in 1942.

They were planning the overthrow of the Nazi regime, yet rejected parliamentary democracy. Stauffenberg and Olbricht jointly coordinated the assassination plans for Hitler and worked out **operation „Valkyrie"** which was officially meant to restore order after internal unrest.

In 1943 Olbricht was made Deputy Commander of the Reserve Army at the Wehrmacht high command, and he succeeded in appointing co-conspirators such as Stauffenberg and Merz von Quirnheim to influential posts in the high command. Hitler, Himmler and Göring were all to be eliminated in the coup.

Thursday, 20 July 1944

7.00: Stauffenberg and his adjutant Werner von Haeften fly from Berlin to the „Wolf's Lair" („Wolfsschanze"), Hitler's headquarters in East Prussia, near Rastenburg. **12.30:** Stauffenberg only manages to activate one of the two time bombs. **12.37:** Stauffenberg enters the conference hut and places his briefcase with the explosives under the large map table in Hitler's vicinity. He leaves the room under a pretext; the briefcase is inadvertently moved aside. **12.42:** the bomb detonates. Of the 24 people present four die. Hitler survives, slightly injured. **12.50:** Stauffenberg leaves the „Wolf's Lair" for Berlin, convinced that Hitler is dead. **15.50:** Friedrich Olbricht sends out the „Valkyrie" order. **18.00:** Goebbels has Hitler's survival in the assassination attempt announced in a radio broadcast. **19.00:** the coup is suppressed. **22.30:** Stauffenberg, Olbricht, von Quirnheim, von Haeften and Ludwig Beck are arrested, court-martialed and shot for high treason.

Civilian Resistance

After Hitler came to power, only disunited resistance developed. Communists worked from the underground, social democrats joined the unions, Lutheran Christians were active in the **„Confessional Church"**, members of the aristocracy and middle classes formed the **„Kreisau Circle"**.

The resistance groups best-known were the students of the **„Weiße Rose"** (White Rose) and the intellectuals and workers of the **„Rote Kapelle"** (Red Chapel). Resistance activities included hiding Jewish citizens, distributing leaflets, acts of sabotage and passing information to the Allies.

30 Memorial to German Resistance

30 Bronze statue in the Bendlerblock courtyard

28
„People's Court"

⌂ Adolf Lohse, 1865 → Bellevue-straße 15, Map B3 Ⓢ Ⓤ Potsdamer Platz From its inception in August 1934 to the end of the war, 4 951 men and women were sentenced to death by a special Court, the so called „People's Court", presided over by especially fanatic Nazi judges and attorneys. The victims were sentenced for treason, defeatism, jokes and doubts about the „final victory" and other „crimes". The hearings against the perpetrators of the July Conspiracy in 1944 took place in the Berlin Supreme Court at Heinrich-von-Kleist Park in Schöneberg. Hitler had already pronounced his judgment and demanded revenge: **„I want them hanged, hanged like animals"**. The infamous president of the „People's Court", Roland Freisler, was addressed by one of the generals accused of the attempt on Hitler's life, Generalfeldmarschall Erwin von Witzleben: **„In three months the tormented German people will call you to account."** That very day von Witzleben was hanged in ▷ Plötzensee Prison.
On 3 February 1945 Freisler was killed during an air raid, as the Supreme Court building collapsed. His successor Harry Haffner continued the court cases with undiminished fanatism. Today, plaques behind the Sony Center and at Kleist Park mark the location of the „People's Court".

29
Euthanasia Center

→ Tiergartenstraße 4–4a, Map B3 Ⓢ Ⓤ Potsdamer Platz Two villas on Tiergartenstraße 4 were used as the Euthanasia Center (codename **„Aktion T4"**). Its official name was **„Reich Committee for the Scientific Registration of Serious Hereditary and Congenitally-Based Diseases"**. From here, the mass murder of psychiatric patients and people in nursing homes was organized. The personnel were moved to Poland in 1943 and were responsible for the management of the extermination camps Chelmno, Belzec, Sobibor and Treblinka.

Under the euthanasia program nearly 200 000 people were killed. The building was severely damaged during the war and razed to the ground in 1950. Today a memorial marks the site.

30
Reich Ministry of War/ Federal Ministry of Defence and Memorial of German Resistance

⌂ Reinhardt & Süßenguth, 1914; Krupp & Druckenmüller, 1938 → Stauffenberg-straße 13–14, Map A4 Ⓢ Ⓤ Potsdamer Platz ⌚ Mon–Wed, Fri 9–18, Thu 9–20, Sat, Sun 10–18 Here, the German generals planned Hitler's war campaigns. But it was also the center of an attempt of military resistance. Here resided the supreme command of the Wehrmacht, under Hitler's direct command since 1938, the supreme command of the army, the air force and the navy, as well as the German counter-intelligence under Admiral Wilhelm Canaris. In the adjacent „Bendlerblock", Hitler addressed the officers on 3 February 1933 in his infamous speech on the „final extermination of Marxism" and the „conquest of new living area in the East and its total Germanization". Here was also the office of the Chief of Staff to the Commander of the Reserve Army, Claus von Stauffenberg. After the failed assassination conspiracy, he and his co-conspirators were court-martialed and shot in the courtyard of the Bendlerblock. The place is marked by a memorial and an exhibition of German resistance against the Nazi regime.

31
„Scars of Remembrance"

→ Sigismundstraße 4, Map B4 Ⓢ Ⓤ Potsdamer Platz Even today many facades in the capital bear the scars of the desperate house-to-house fighting during the Battle of Berlin in April 1945. Grenades and machine gun bullets have left these scars. Here, they have been conserved impressively during the building's recent restoration. The building itself today is part of the National Gallery of Paintings.

32
Embassy of Italy
⌂ Friedrich Hetzelt, 1938–1941
→ Tiergartenstraße 21a–23, Map A3
Ⓢ Ⓤ Potsdamer Platz For the construction of the ▷ Great Hall, a number of embassies around the Reichstag were pulled down.
Speer envisaged a new „Diplomats' District" at Tiergarten, where all embassies would be concentrated.
The Italian embassy was the first to be built in 1938.
Size and design were supposed to embody the importance of the alliance of fascist Italy with Nazi Germany.
Shortly after completion, the building was damaged in an air raid and only rebuilt in the 1990s.
In contrast to the „Third Reich" administrative buildings now used by federal ministries, here the symbols of power of Italian fascism have strangely enough been preserved according to conservationist guidelines.

33
Embassy of Japan
⌂ Ludwig Moshamer, 1938–1942
→ Tiergartenstraße 24–27, Map A3
Ⓢ Ⓤ Potsdamer Platz
As part of the redesign of the Reich capital, the Japanese embassy as well as the Italian embassy were relocated to the newly created „Diplomats' District".
The representational building of one of the members of the Berlin-Rome-Tokyo Axis shows a monumental design similar to Nazi architecture. Heavily damaged in the war, the building remained a ruin for a long time. The façade is original, while the interior was completely rebuilt.

34
Psychiatric Clinic and Mental Hospital of the Charité
⌂ Georg Diestel & Georg Thül, 1710
→ Bonhoefferweg 3, Map C1
Ⓢ Ⓤ Friedrichstraße
The oldest medical training institute in Germany was originally built as a plague house. King Frederick Wilhelm I decreed that the building was to be named the Haus Charité (House of Charity).
When the Nazis came to power in 1933, at least 145 doctors of the Charité were dismissed for „racial" and „political" reasons. Many of the internationally renowned Physics had to leave the country to save their lives, while others were killed in the Theresienstadt concentration camp.
From 1938 to 1945, the Nazi psychiatrist Maximilian de Crinis was the director of the university hospital. Since 1939, the SS Hauptsturmführer had been the „éminence grise" in the organizational staff of the ▷ Euthanasia Center and the „Aktion T4" and the driving force behind the killing of psychiatric patients. According to Nazi doctrine, unrestrained research on mental patients was allowed.
After the war about 20 percent of the Charité lay in ruins. Today, the campus of the university hospital is an oasis of silence, and houses, among others, the medical museum founded by Rudolf Virchow, at Schuhmannstraße 20/21. Thousands of exhibits of the pathological collection were lost in the war, but it still is one of the most comprehensive of its kind in the world.

35
Reich Railways Bunker
⌂ Karl Bonatz, 1943
→ Albrechtstraße 24–25, Map D1
Ⓢ Ⓤ Friedrichstraße
Its exposed situation may account for the elaborate facade design. This fortress-like monolith provided shelter for about 3000 people behind its walls of 1.8 meters and a ceiling of more than 3 meters.
In 1946, the Allied Control Authority decreed the demolition of all buildings that might be used for military purposes. Because of proximity to public housing, not all bunkers above ground could be blown up.
This bunker was later used as storage place for potatoes and then became a techno club. Today, the building is under preservation order and is used as a venue for art exhibitions.

33 Japanese Embassy

38 Federal eagle at the Foreign Office

32 Italian Embassy

43 New Synagogue

42 Sculpture for the Commemoration of Deported Jews

34 Entrance to the Mental Hospital of the Charité

36 New Guard House in winter with the statue by Käthe Kollwitz

37 Memorial to the Burning of Books

41 „Stumbling Stones" – commemorating deported Jews

41 Workshop for the blind

36
New Guard House
⌂ Karl-Friedrich Schinkel, 1818
→ Unter den Linden 4, Map E2
Ⓤ Hausvogteiplatz In the 1920s architect Heinrich Tessenow redesigned the interior of the guardhouse as a memorial hall for the victims of the First World War.
The Nazis turned it into a **hall of fame for heroes**; during GDR times, it was the home of the **Memorial for the Victims of Fascism and Militarism**. Since 1993 the New Guardhouse is the official **memorial of the Federal Republic of Germany for the „Victims of War and Tyranny"**.

37
Monument to the Burning of Books, Memorial „Underground Library"
⌂ Micha Ullmann, 1995 → Bebelplatz, Map E3 Ⓤ Hausvogteiplatz
„This was a prelude only; where books are burnt, people will be burning in the end." This statement by Jewish poet Heinrich Heine in 1820 was to be proved right in the most gruesome form. On 10 May 1933, students in SA uniforms, led by the Minister for Propaganda, Joseph Goebbels, marched to Opernplatz (Bebelplatz) under the slogan: **German Students against the un-German Spirit**.
In a pyre 20 000 books were „consigned to the flames". Among the authors now banned were
· Bertolt Brecht
· Albert Einstein
· Lion Feuchtwanger
· Sigmund Freud
· Maxim Gorki
· Heinrich Heine
· Franz Kafka
· Erich Kästner
· Jack London
· Thomas Mann
· Karl Marx
· Walter Rathenau
· Erich Maria Remarque
· Kurt Tucholsky
· Voltaire
· H.G. Wells
· Émile Zola.

From this date, Goebbels regularly published a list of authors whose works had to be removed from bookshops and public libraries.

38
Reich Bank/ Ministry of Foreign Affairs
⌂ Heinrich Wolff, 1934–1938 → Werderscher Markt 1, Map E3 Ⓤ Hausvogteiplatz In 1933 a competition for the extension of the Reich Bank was held. Martin Gropius and Mies van der Rohe took part, but Adolf Hitler decided personally to give the commission to the Director of Buildings of the Reich Bank, Heinrich Wolff. With its 60 000 square meters of usable space it became one of the largest administrative buildings in Berlin. The bank safes held the confiscated possessions of Jewish citizens, later including the gold teeth of Jews killed in the concentration and extermination camps. Precious metal, looted by the Wehrmacht all over Europe, was melted down in Berlin, and, to disguise its origin, the ingots were stamped with the date 1935. During the socialist GDR era, it was the seat of the SED Party's Central Committee. The building today houses the Federal Ministry of Foreign Affairs.

39
Karl-Liebknecht-House
⌂ Keibel, 1912 → Kleine Alexanderstraße 28, Map F1 Ⓤ Rosa-Luxemburg-Platz On 23 February 1933, SA troops seized this house, which the Communist Party of Germany had bought in 1926, and renamed it „Horst Wessel House" after one of the Nazivictims of street fighting in Berlin. The „Department for the Fight against Bolshevism" was set up here, where police forces tortured political opponents and Jews.
Today the building houses the PDS, the successor of the GDR state party SED and former communist party KPD, and has reverted to its original name, „Karl Liebknecht House" (a leader of the German workers movement at the beginning of the 20th century, killed in 1919 by right-wing soldiers).

Traces of German-Je

40
Social Welfare Office of the Jewish Community

⌂ Johann Hoeniger, 1906 → Rosenstraße 2–4, Map F2 Ⓢ Ⓤ Alexanderplatz In 1943 the Gestapo rounded up about 1700 Jewish men, married to „Aryan" women, and took them to the Rosenstraße assembly point before deportation. Some of the wives gathered at the building and demanded their husbands' release. More and more women joined this unique protest demonstration, which continued for a week. Probably on Goebbel's orders, most of the men were finally released. An information pillar and a sculpture recall the events, which in 2003 were made into a film by Margarethe von Trotta, called „Rosenstraße".

41
Workshop for the Blind

→ Hackescher Markt 41–43, Map F1 Ⓢ Hackescher Markt ⊘ Mo–Fr 12–20, Sa, So 11–20 The owner of a brush workshop, Otto Weidt, managed to declare 27 deaf and blind Jews as essential for war production up until February 1943. During the SS-„Operation Factory" they were finally deported to „extermination camps" in the east. Weidt was able to hide a whole Jewish family for another nine months, before they were deported to Auschwitz as well. The original workshop is now a small museum.

42
Jewish Boys' School

⌂ Johann Hoeniger, 1906 → Große Hamburger Straße 27, Map F1 Ⓢ Hackescher Markt From the middle of the 17th century, the Grosse Hamburger Straße was an important center of Jewish life in Berlin. On 30 June 1942 the Gestapo seized the building and turned it into an infamous assembly and transit camp. The neighbouring old people's home suffered an equally horrendous fate. About 55 000 Jewish citizens of Berlin were herded into similar „Jewish camps" before being deported to the concentration camps or ghettos.

45
Ministerial Gardens/Memorial to the Murdered Jews of Europe (Holocaust Memorial)

⌂ Peter Eisenman, 2005 → Ebertstraße, Map C3 Ⓢ Unter den Linden Inaugurated on 10 May 2005, the Memorial to the Murdered Jews of Europe, comprising an area of 20 000 square meters, was built at the site of the former Ministerial

Gardens, the gardens behind the ministry buildings along Wilhelm Street.

Hidden underground: Joseph

2 711 concrete pillars arranged in a grid, form a field of steles, up to five

wish history in Berlin

Behind the old people's home used to be Berlin's oldest Jewish cemetery until 1943. The Nazis destroyed it completely, breaking up thousands of gravestones. Today, the reconstructed gravestone of Moses Mendelssohn marks the site of the former graveyard.

The old people's home was demolished after the war, while the former school building was made a Jewish school again in 1991.

43
New Synagogue /
Centrum Judaicum

⌂ Knoblauch, Stüler, 1866 → Oranienburger Straße 28–30, Map E1 Ⓢ Oranienburger Straße ⏲ Sun–Thu 10–18, Fri 10–14 During the pogrom of 9 November 1938, the complete destruction of the largest and most magnificent Jewish prayer house was miraculously prevented by police officer Wilhelm Krützfeld.

He drew his pistol to drive away the SA arsonists and called the fire brigade. The fact that they came and put out the fire was another extraordinary event on that day. The general order was to act only if the fire threatened neighbouring non-Jewish buildings. In 1943 the synagogue was severely damaged during an air raid and partly reconstructed in 1988 by GDR government. Since 1995 the building is the home of the Centrum Judaicum with an archive of the history and culture of the Jewish Berliners.

Only a few of the 14 Berlin synagogues survived the November pogrom and the war; today there are six altogether in the city.

44
Jewish Hospital

⌂ Eduard Knoblauch, 1861 → Auguststraße 14–16, Map E1 Ⓢ Oranienburger Straße After the original hospital was forced to move to larger premises, a number of Jewish welfare organizations were housed in this building. From 1941 to 1943 the Gestapo used it as another assembly point for Berlin Jews selected for deportation to the camps. The building is currently empty.

meters high and accessible at any point. In 1997, at the start of the building

Joseph Goebbels' private bunker. The propaganda minister's town villa used to be here, and he had used the bunker up to april 1945, when, during the Battle of Berlin, the Scandinavian SS-"Nordland" division made it their command center.

The proposal to integrate the bunker into the „Holocaust Memorial" was not taken up by the city council.

ebbels' sealed private bunker

works, workers discovered a layer of concrete 2 meters thick: the ceiling of

South Station

Tempelhof Airfield

Arch of Triumph

North-South-Axis

Army Supreme Command

Reich Marshal's Office

Victory Column

Brandenburg Gate

Reichstag

„Führer's Palace"

Great Hall

Great Basin

Town Hall

Navy Supreme Command

North Station

World Capital „Germania"

Berlin's tranformation into the future world capital of the „Great German Reich" was intended to be finished by 1950, after the „final victory", when Berlin should have been ceremonially renamed **„Germania"**. The new capital was supposed to be a **„fitting expression of the greatness of its mission"** according to Hitler. Albert Speer, Hitler's favourite architect was commissioned to prepare the plans. As Inspector General for Buildings for the Reich Capital Berlin, he was placed under Hitlers personal command. As well as Berlin, about 40 other so-called „cities of the Führer" were to be redesigned with monumental buildings and boulevards. The focal point and highlight of the redesigned Berlin was to be the Great Hall, 320 meters high, crowned with a dome and providing space for up to 180 000 people. To the south of it and crossing the east-west axis, a boulevard, five kilometers long and 120 meters wide, was to feature grand offices, palaces and a gigantic „Arch of Triumph" on the north-south axis. Two enormous train stations in the north and the south were to be linked via ring roads and an underground train system, while at the four axial points on the outskirts of the city four airfields were planned. According to Speer's „theory of ruin value", the most important buildings were to be built from granite, following classical tradition, so that even a thousand years hence, the ruins, like those of ancient Rome, would tell the story of a heroic past. Hitler claimed to have worked on the designs for the comprehensive modernization of Berlin already during his imprisonment in Landsberg in 1924. In 1936 he showed Speer his sketchbook with the words: **„I made those drawings some ten years ago. I have kept them because I never doubted that I would build them. And now we will make it happen."** The demolition of large areas of central Berlin and a ruthless clearance policy were the pre-requisites for the start of the building program. According to Speer's proposal, more than 70 000 Berlin Jews were forcibly evicted in what was euphemistically called „de-tenanting measures", while thousands of concentration camp prisoners were put to work in quarries for the gigantic project, also on Speer's request.

Left: The model of the future world capital „Germania", length 30 m, used by Adolf Hitler and Albert Speer for the complete reshaping of Berlin, vista towards the south.
Bottom: Plan for the main lecture hall of the future university campus.

Great Hall

⌂ Albert Speer, 1936 → Adolf-Hitler-Square/Platz der Republik In 1936, based on Hitler's sketch from the 1920s, Speer began designing the domed structure.
The hall, resting on a square base 315 meters wide and with a height of 320 meters, would carry on top a 40 meters lantern, crowned with an eagle atop the swastika.

In 1939 Hitler told Speer: **„This has to be changed. Instead of the swastika, the eagle is to be perched above the globe. To crown this greatest building in the world, the eagle must stand above the globe."**
Up to 180 000 people would have fitted into the hall, seated on platforms 30 meters high, listening to the „Führer's" endless diatribes from his balcony underneath the gilded Reich eagle, towering 14 meters high.

The dome would have been clearly visible above low clouds, providing an ideal target for enemy bombers. But Hitler at that time was convinced that no enemy bomber ever would reach Berlin.

In 1938, encouraged on by Hitler, who wanted to see the hall finished during his lifetime, Speer began the demolition work around the ▷ **Reichstag**, and bought huge amounts of granite and marble all over Europe. The inauguration was planned for 1950, but, at the end of the war, all that was left of the grandiose plans was a ditch full of ground water.

„Führer's Palace",
Adolf Hitler Square

⌂ Albert Speer, 1942 → Adolf-Hitler-Platz/Kanzleramt, Platz der Republik

In November 1938, before the ▷ **New Reich Chancellery** was finished, plans existed for yet another „Führer's Palace", Hitler's future official residence in Berlin. Situated to the west of the ▷ **Great Hall**, the fortress-like building with its windowless façade would have covered at least 2 million square meters, including the surrounding parks. State visitors would have passed through an immense gate into the Court of Honour, 110 meters long.

A series of colonnaded courtyards would have led to magnificent reception rooms, galleries and banqueting halls. The longest flight of rooms was to be the so-called „diplomats' promenade" of 500 meters, leading to Hitler's study and giving the visitor the impression

320 meters: megalomania in stone

320 m
310 m
300 m
290 m
280 m
270 m
260 m
250 m
240 m
230 m
220 m
210 m
200 m
190 m
180 m
170 m
160 m
150 m
140 m
130 m
120 m
110 m
100 m
90 m
80 m
70 m
60 m
50 m
40 m
30 m
20 m
10 m

that he was being received by the **ruler of the world**. Next to the study, itself the size of a station hall, would have been his private rooms.

The „Adolf Hitler Square" in front of the palace was to accommodate up to one million people. Sensing that people's support might not last for ever, Hitler according to Speer mused: „**It is not out of the question that I shall one day be forced to adopt unpopular measures. These might possibly lead to riots. We must provide for this eventuality. All**

levels. In the center would have been a huge gallery from which the „Reich Marshall" wanted to announce his **„motto of the year"** to the assembled officers of the Nazi Airforce. The flat roof with its 11800 square meters was to be covered with soil, making a garden in the air with swimming pool, tennis court and fountains plus an amphitheater for 240 spectators.

Speer planned a similar building, though smaller in size, for himself on Lichtenstein Alley in the Tiergarten district of

„The capital has to adapt to the greatness of its mission." (Adolf Hitler)

the buildings on this square must be equipped with heavy steel bulletproof shutters over their windows. The doors, too, must be of steel, and there should be heavy iron gates for closing off the square. It must be possible to defend the center of the Reich like a fortress." To the south of „Adolf Hitler Square" was to be the new final **„Reich Chancellery"** and the „Supreme Command of the Wehrmacht", framing the entrance to the square. On its east side would have been the now dwarfed ▷ **Reichstag**, extended with a new parliamentary building that was to house the few sessions of the Nazi party assemblies.

Reich Marshall's Office
⌂ Albert Speer, 1939 → Große Straße/ Entlastungsstraße Feeling somewhat neglected in his newly built ▷ **Reich Aviation Ministry**, Hermann Göring commissioned Speer with a new design to match the monumental buildings along the envisioned north-south axis. Speer understood the ambitions of Göring all too well. He designed a building that was pretty close in style and splendour to the new ▷ **„Führer's Palace"** next to the ▷ **Great Hall**. The building, 240 meters long, was to have the grandest stair hall in the world with rows of columns over several

Berlin. He obtained two villas formerly owned by exiled jews and had them transformed into one modern administrative building for his private architectural company, which executed the buildings commissioned to him by Hitler (thus Speer had become a multimillionaire by the end of the war).

„Soldiers' Hall"
⌂ Wilhelm Kreis, 1941 → Große Straße/ Entlastungsstraße The „Soldiers' Hall" was to be the central memorial to the German soldiers killed in the Second World War. Architect Wilhelm Kreis, who planned similar memorials along the borders of the future „Greater German Reich", envisaged a vault underneath the vast hall. In a **„Sacred Crypt"**, made from unpolished granite and lit only by huge flaming vessel, the sarcophagus of Frederick the Great as well as famous German field marshals like Erwin Rommel were to find their final resting place.

In the exhibition halls above, visitors would have been able to view precious trophies of war. According to Hitler's ideas, one of the main trophies was to be the famous railway car from Compiègne in which in 1918 the German surrender and in 1940 the armistice with France had been signed.

North Station and Great Basin

⌂ Dierksmeier, Bastelmeyer, Bonatz & Dübbers, 1941 → Großes Becken/ Hamburger Bahnhof The North Railway Station was to be more or less identical in size to its southern counterpart. Travelers exiting via the grand staircase would have looked on the „Great Basin" with its reflections of the Great Hall. Along the complete length of the east bank the „High Command of the Navy" was to be built. Opposite, a city forum with the new Berlin town hall and the police headquarters were planned.

Arch of Triumph

⌂ Albert Speer, 1939 → Große Straße/ Kolonnenbrücke **„Based on the Führer's ideas"**, as stated on the plans, Albert Speer designed the „Arch of Triumph", 117 meters high, 170 meters wide and 119 meters deep, situated at the southern end of the north-south axis, the counter point to the Great Hall. With a volume of 2.5 million cubic meters, the arch, respectfully referred to as **„Structure T"**, would have been 50 times larger than the „Arc de Triomphe" in Paris. Hitler wanted the granite walls to carry the names of all the German soldiers killed in the First World War. On 20 April 1939, Speer present- ed Hitler on his 50th birthday with a 4-meter model of the arch, which Hitler had sketch- ed in the 1920s. The „Füh- rer" was deeply touched ... Today, on the grounds of the planned arch, the

▷ **„Großbelastungskörper"** („Heavy Load Testing Body"), a relic of the „Germania" world metropolis redevelopment plans still exists. Speer had commissioned this huge piece of concrete in 1941 to test for settlement on the building site.

South Railway Station, War Trophy Boulevard

⌂ Albert Speer, 1940 → Große Straße/ General-Pape-Straße To make sufficient space for the „north-south-axis", all rail traffic would have had to disappear from the center of Berlin. Therefore the first project (to be realized by 1945) was the South Railway Station. The dimensions of the gigantic building of steel and glass would have eclipsed even Grand Central Station in New York. Travelers would have arrived on four levels and exited via the grand flight of stairs to the monumental

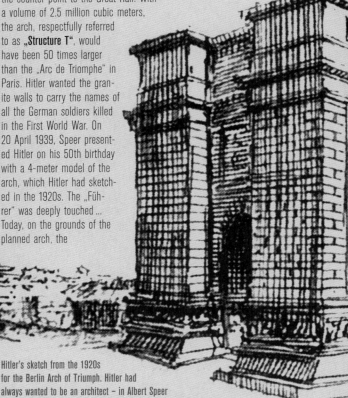

Hitler's sketch from the 1920s for the Berlin Arch of Triumph. Hitler had always wanted to be an architect – in Albert Speer he found the ideal person to execute his monumental building plans.

station square of 1000 meters length, which was to exhibit the weapons captured in victorious battles. Visitors would have had an uninterrupted view of the dome of the ▷**Great Hall**, five kilometers away, framed by the ▷**„Arch of Triumph"**.

University Campus

⌂ Albert Speer, 1938–1943 → Heerstraße Between the already finished ▷**Olympic Grounds** and the river Havel, a grandiose university campus was to be developed as the western gate to the metropolis „Germania". Along Heerstraße an ensemble of lecture halls and research laboratories was planned by Speer and his architects.

To replace the Charité, which was to make way for the building of the ▷**Great Hall**, a new university hospital was to be built here too. The visual center of the complex was the enormous lecture hall, crowned with flaming vessels at its corner columns.

Military Sciences Faculty / Teufelsberg

⌂ Hans Malwitz, 1937 → Teufelsberg, Grunewald Ⓢ Heerstraße In 1948, the amount of rubble and debris in Berlin – due to war and fighting – was estimated to be around 60 to 70 million cubic meters. Some of it, around 2 million bricks salvaged by Berlin's 60000 **„Trümmerfrauen"** (rubble women), was reused for the reconstruction of Berlin. The „Teufelsberg" (Devil's Mountain) is one of 16 rubble mountains and with its 120 meters the highest elevation in Berlin. Underneath the 13 million cubic meters of rubble is the shell of the „Military Sciences Faculty" and its extensive shelters. In 1937, Hitler set the foundation stone for the fortress-like complex that later was to include an Army Ordnance Office designed by Wilhelm Kreis. The nearby Grunewald Forest was to become something like the „Bois de Boulogne" in Paris with stables, restaurants and recreation sites. Here, between 1948 and 1990, the US Army ran one of the largest espionage posts in Germany, featuring monitoring operations as far as Moscow.

Albert Speer 1905–1981

At 29 years of age, the young architect from Mannheim had arrived at the center of power in Berlin. As successor to Paul Ludwig Troost he became the „Führer's architect" in 1934 and was responsible for the Nazi's gigantic building plans.

In 1937 Hitler appointed him „Inspector General for Buildings in the Reich Capital Berlin" and commissioned him with the plans for the transformation of Berlin into the world capital „Germania".

Speer had proved his organizational talents at various mass events of the Nazi party. He was also the architect of the ▷ New Reich Chancellery in Voss-Street (built from 1936 to 1939). After his visit to conquered Paris in 1940, Hitler boasted: „When we are done with Berlin, Paris will be only a shadow".

But war changed all this. In 1942, as Reich Minister of Armaments and Munitions, Speer became the second powerful man after Hitler. He was now master of millions of forced laborers and the whole of the German war industry, which he led with military discipline. Armaments production in the 5th year of the war climbed to new heights, despite allied bombers laying waste to Germany's cities. Important production sites were moved underground.

In the final days of the war, Speer had some of the first rockets and jet planes built. Attacks on the USA with transcontinental rockets A9/A10 were planned, and Speer hoped to arm them with the new poison gas Sarin or with a „uranium bomb".

In the spring of 1945 Speer refused to comply with Hitler's orders to destroy all industrial plants and infrastructure, leaving nothing but scorched earth for the advancing Allies.

At the Nuremberg trials, Speer was one of the few who confessed a general guilt for the crimes of the Nazis, while vigorously denying any personal guilt. Speer served his 20-year sentence at ▷ Spandau prison in Berlin. Here he wrote his selfcomplacent autobiography, and he paced the prison courtyard, counting each step. In his mind he thus walked thousands of kilometers into the world. On the eve of his release, he would have crossed half the globe and therefore telegraphed to his friend Rudolf Wolters: „Please pick up 530 km south of Guadalajara, Mexico. Uncle Alex."

Mussolini Square and Station

⌂ Albert Speer, 1940 → Mussolini-platz/Theodor-Heuss-Platz Ⓢ Ⓤ Theodor-Heuss-Platz Since 1933 the former „Reichskanzler Square" (today „Theodor Heuss Square") was named after Adolf Hitler. To honour the Italian dictator, the square was to be renamed Mussolini Square in 1938. The highest elevation on the east-west axis was to be surrounded by two circular arcades, more than 10 meters high, in its center a prominent tower crowned by a sculpture. The **citytrain station Heerstraße**, where Hitler had welcomed Mussolini in 1937, was to be the reception station for state visitors and was also to be renamed after the „Duce".

Berlin's New Southern Suburb

⌂ Albert Speer, 1941 → Rangsdorf Away from the center of Berlin, towards the east and south, extensive residential areas for up to 210 000 inhabitants were planned as well as industrial districts. This specific area stretched from South Railway Station, as a meridional continuation of the north-south axis, for 16 km as far as the Berlin highway ring. Here the „High Command of the Waffen-SS" was planned: a high-rise tower with gigantic „SS" letters, the War Academy of the Army, the Reich archives, a Reich customs service academy, a stadium with parade grounds plus large barracks designed by architect Werner March (who had already pinned the Olympic Stadium). Behind the monumental administrative buildings, housing areas were planned, thinning out into single-family homes and villas towards the edge of the city. The terminal point of the south axis was to be the south airfield on the banks of the Rangsdorfer Lake, where also large flying boats would have been able to land.

Relics of „Germania" in Berlin:
▷ Victory Column ▷ Streetlights on Straße des 17. Juni ▷ Embassy of Italy ▷ Embassy of Japan ▷ Embassy of Yugoslavia ▷ Heavy Load Testing Body ▷ Workers' City Great Hall ▷ „Speer-Plate/Panel"

Interior of the Soldiers' Hall, 63 m high

„Führer's Palace"

„When we are done with Berlin, Paris will be only a shadow."

(Hitler to Speer when visiting conquered Paris)

View through the Arch of Triumph on to Adolf Hitler Square

Manoeuvers on the 30 m long model street

Isolated Brandenburg Gate

„I was fascinated by this opportunity to build without any restrictions."

(Albert Speer)

Military Academy

Albert Speer at Pariser Platz, 1942

The Bombing Raids on Berlin

From „**Germania**" to Gomorrah – more bombs were dropped on Berlin than on any other city during the Second World War. Hitler did not show himself overly concerned about this fact, remarking to Speer: „**Our new plan would have meant the demolition of 80 000 houses in Berlin. Unfortunately the British haven't done their work quite according to your plans. But a start has been made.**" At the end of the war, the capital was a sea of ruins.

The German air force had first proved how devastating an attack by air could be with the bombing of Guernica (Spain) and later with bombing raids on Warsaw, Rotterdam and Coventry. During the Battle of Britain, pilots were initially ordered to attack military targets only. But later, during the „Blitz", as the British press called the German air raids on London and other British towns, residential areas, particularly in London, were targeted as well.

On 26 August 1940 the British Bomber Command conducted its first counter attack on the Reich capital Berlin. 50 planes took part in the raid. The result: some hits on the outskirts of Berlin and thousands of leaflets dropped over Berlin. Since November 1943, Berlin was the target of massive air attacks. The German air defense, involving up to 900 000 men and women, was able to withstand more or less until the summer of 1944. A dense network of anti-aircraft batteries and searchlights awaited the allied bomber units at the Atlantic coast. For the defense of Berlin, three huge ▷ **Flak Towers** were built in the center, at **Humboldthain, Friedrichshain** and at Berlin **Zoo**. Each of those fortresses of 2.5 m thick reinforced concrete, provided protection for at least 22 000 people from the now daily hail of bombs. Rising 42 m above ground level, on the roof platform stood four twin anti-aircraft batteries, the most efficient of World War II. A second, smaller bunker tower, providing shelter for another 8 000 people, served as

> „**I think this war virus is so deep in the Germans that maybe at the end of the war we'll have to castrate all the German men so they won't keep on reproducing people who want to make war.**" (Franklin D. Roosevelt)

USA: 22 800 tons

Britain: 45 500 tons

68000 tons of bombs were dropped on Berlin, 35000 people lost their lives.

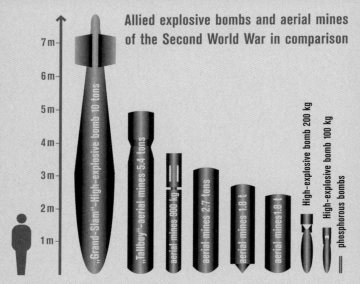

Allied explosive bombs and aerial mines of the Second World War in comparison

7 m
6 m
5 m
4 m
3 m
2 m
1 m

„Grand-Slam"-High-explosive bomb 10 tons

„Tallboy"-aerial mines 5.4 tons

aerial mines 900 kg

aerial mines 2.7 tons

aerial mines 1.8 t

aerial mines 1.8 t

High-explosive bomb 200 kg

High-explosive bomb 100 kg

phosphorous bombs

Apart from the atom bomb, the British „Grand Slam" at nearly 10 tons and with a height of 7.7 meters was probably the biggest bomb of the Second World War. Before impact it reached sonic speed. The 7 m thick ceiling of the U-boat shelter „Valentin" in Bremen was severely damaged and penetrated after two hits. The Grand Slam was used 41 times after 14 March 1945, and 854 aerial mines of the Tallboy type were dropped.

command center. But in the end, the Allied supremacy was such that the destruction of most German cities could not be prevented.

This was also due to a series of miscalculations on Hitler's part. He had the first jet airplane, the Messerschmitt 262, remodeled as a bomber, instead of using it as a jet fighter against the „flying fortresses" of the Allied forces. Hitler also halted the production of the ground-to-air missile „Waterfall", to speed up the development of the Reprisal Weapon 2 (Vergeltungswaffe V2), which proved to be worthless from a military point of view (even though the psychological impact was enormous).

American B-17 bombers dropping their deadly load over the „Reich"

The Firestorm

In Berlin, the Allied forces did not succeed in igniting a firestorm as they did in Hamburg, Pforzheim or Dresden. Berlin's broader streets, brickstone houses, numerous parks and canals prevented an extended fire. In towns with a medieval center (wooden houses), conflagrations killed tens of thousands of people. A sophisticated sequence of different bombs produced the inferno:

1. Huge aerial mines with up to 10 tons of explosives, so-called **blockbusters**, removed whole roofs, demolished windows and walls with their enormous blast wave.

2. Hundreds of thousands of small stick-type incendiary bombs or phosphorous bombs then rained onto the target, creating a sea of flames in the draught produced by the exploded houses.

3. High-explosive bombs finished off the task. Sometimes equipped with timers, they exploded hours after the air raid, killing the fire brigade and ambulance people. The individual fires united to create a firestorm, using up so much oxygen that people were suffocated in their shelters.

Such „carpet bombing" was directed mainly against German morale, not against any direct military target. The technique of killing, systematically planned and executed, its victims now Hitler's friends and foes alike, had been thoroughly researched by Allied scientists. On a secret test site in the desert of Utah, 1 to 1 copies of Berlin blocks of flats had been erected for practice purposes.

Air Marshal Arthur „Bomber" Harris, who had promised the British „to bomb Berlin until the heart of Nazi-Germany has ceased beating", devised „Operation Thunderclap" to wipe out the Reich capital. In coordination with US forces, the British planned to kill and injure up to 220 000 Berliners in one attack, concentrating explicitly on residential areas. On 3 February 1945, 2 000 B-17 bombers of the 8th USAAF unloaded phosphorous and explosives bombs over Berlin. Nearly a quarter of the inner city districts were demolished, about 1.5 million people lost their homes and tens of thousands died in the hail of bombs. In the wake of such attacks, the Nazi secret service noted a certain defiance within the population.
Senses were numbed, people drew closer together and suffered their fate.

Tracer paths of German Anti Aircraft Guns in the Berlin night sky, 1943

Bombed-out people didn't think about resistance to Hitler but about food and shelter.

> „Your heart misses a beat,
> reading about the air raids
> on Berlin ... They are not linked
> to military operations, so you
> don't see an end to the war,
> but an end to Germany."
>
> (Bertolt Brecht, 1943)

Nazi organizations provided the home-less with essential support (e.g. furniture taken away from Jewish families) and opened up soup kitchens to feed the population. The building program for shelters was intensified.
The Allies' plan to stimulate resistance against Hitler did not succeed.

At the end of the war, large parts of the capital were destroyed. 612 000 homes and one fifth of all buildings no longer ex-isted. The heap of rubble that used to be Berlins now destroyed buildings consisted of 70 million cubic meters piled up in several rubble mountains. More than 35 000 people died in over 360 air raids.

Churchill even considered using biological weapons such as anthrax and wanted to flood **Germany with poison gas if necessary**.
In the end he ordered 500 000 **N-Bombs** containing anthrax from Roosevelt. They were kept ready in case Germany would use similar weapons. Hitler planned to attack the USA with the **„America Missile"** A9/A10, developed by SS-engineer Wernher von Braun and his colleagues in Peenemünde. New York was to be razed to the ground to **„teach the Jews a lesson with terror attacks on the big cities"**.

In Germany alone, about 600 000 people were killed by the nearly 1.5 million tons of explosive and incendiary bombs dropped by the Allied forces during the Second World War.
The number of people missing has never been established. Half of the 7 000 Lancaster bombers flying over Germany were shot down; 55 000 crewmembers were killed.

Remains of the Bombing Raids:
> ▷ Kaiser Wilhelm Memorial Church
> ▷ Anhalter Station & Shelter
> ▷ Reich Railways Shelter
> ▷ Anti Aircraft Bunker Friedrichshain
>   & Humboldthain
> ▷ Underground Shelters
> ▷ Air-Raid Shelter Gesundbrunnen
> ▷ Allied Museum Teufelsberg
> ▷ Airforce Museum of the German
>   Federal Armed Forces

The Battle of Berlin

On 16 April 1945, nearly six years after its beginning, the Second World War returned to its place of origin with the Battle of Berlin. Millions of German, Italian and Japanese Soldiers had waged war on one seventh of the world's surface. The result: 60 million dead, 50 million injured, 20 million refugees and 80 000 towns and villages destroyed. After the encircling of Berlin by the Red Army, the air raids ceased, but during the bitter house-to-house fighting the dying continued. Thousands more lives were lost in the senseless defense of the Reich capital.

On 9 March 1945, Hitler issued his order for the defense of Berlin: „The Reich capital will be defended to the last man and the last bullet.“ The defense circle surrounded Berlin in a radius of over 60 km and was divided into eight zones. The inner circle around the ▷ New Reich Chancellery and Hitler's last headquarters, the ▷ „Führer Bunker“, was called „Citadel“.

On the dawn of the 16 April 1945 the attack by Soviet troops at the Seelow heights on the banks of the river Oder, 70 km east of Berlin, began. At this final natural barrier guarding Berlin, about 200 000 German soldiers and a division of deserters were gathered. They were confronted by 900 000 advancing Red Army soldiers.

In attacks that incurred heavy losses, the Soviet troops under Marshal Georgi K. Zhukov managed to break through on 17 April. About 70 000 Red Army soldiers and 12 000 German soldiers were killed. In a pincer movement, 2.5 million Soviet soldiers and their 6 000 tanks, 41 000 guns and mortars plus 7500 planes advanced towards the capital. They were opposed by half a million German soldiers: remnants of the Wehrmacht, members of the Waffen-SS, „Volkssturm“ (Public Storm, the last levy), police and „Hitler Youth“. A few hundred tanks and a handful of planes, suffering from severe shortage of fuel and ammunition, were all the defendents had left.

On 20 April, Hitler celebrated his last birthday in the „Führer Bunker“, most of the other Nazi leaders fled the capital shortly afterwards. On the following day the first Red Army troops crossed the city limits and advanced towards the center.

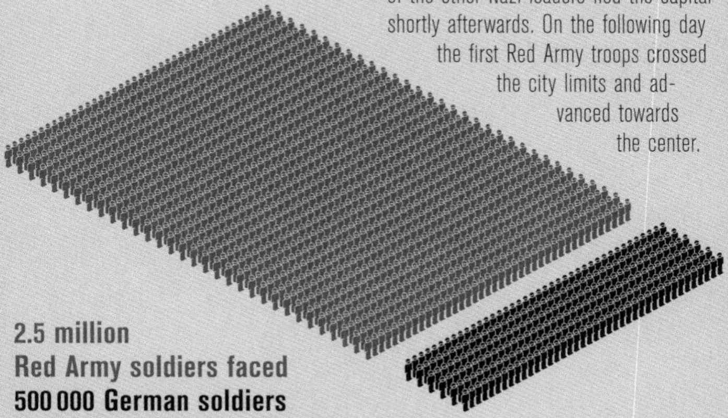

**2.5 million
Red Army soldiers faced
500 000 German soldiers
in the Battle of Berlin.**

Führerbefehl.

An die Berliner Bevölkerung!

Merkt Euch, jeder, der die Maßnahmen, die unsere Widerstandskraft schwächen, propagiert oder gar billigt, ist ein Verräter! Er ist augenblicklich zu erschießen oder zu erhängen! Das gilt auch dann, wenn angeblich solche Maßnahmen im Auftrag des Gauleiters Reichsminister Dr. Göbbels oder gar im Namen des Führers befohlen werden sollten.

gez. Adolf Hitler

22. April 1945

The fire of the huge **Anti Aircraft Guns** on the ▷**Flak Towers** in Friedrichshain, **Humboldhain** and at the Berlin **Zoo** was no longer directed to the sky but at the Soviet tanks advancing in the streets. On 25 April the capital was more or less encircled. After bitter fighting in Reinickendorf, Wedding, Prenzlauer Berg, Tempelhof and Friedrichshain, the Soviets conquered Kreuzberg Heights on 26 April and were able to look down on their real target, the ▷**Reichstag**. The following day saw heavy fighting in Charlottenburg, Wilmersdorf, Tiergarten and the Museum Isle in the center, while Spandau, in the west of the city, already had capitulated.
On 29 April the Red Army reached the desperately defended government district. Hitler had put SS Major General

---

„We might go under. But we will take a world with us."
(Hitler in April 1945)

Wilhelm Mohnke under his personal command and put him in charge of the defense sector „Citadel" around the ▷**Reich Chancellery**. Ironically, among the defenders of this area there were hardly any Germans left. Remnants of the French „Charlemagne" SS-division and combined units of the Scandinavian „Nordland" SS-division, Dutch and Latvian SS units were among the most determined defenders. They had never taken prisoners and they did not expect a different fate for themselves.

„Victory or Siberia",

was written on house façades. This was a fight to total destruction, ordered by the German generals in command. Their end was also to be the end of the German people. When even Hitler realized that defeat was inevitable and that **Wenck's „Miracle Army"** would never reach Berlin, he committed suicide in the ▷ **„Führer Bunker"** on 30 April 1945. His followers either took their own lives or tried to flee from the impending nemesis. In the early hours of the 2 May 1945 the Supreme Commander of the Defense Area Berlin, General Helmuth Weidling, issued his last order: **„On 30 April the ‚Führer' took his own life, leaving us who have sworn allegiance**

Armoured personnel carrier of the Scandinavian SS-division „Nordland" in Chausseestraße. April 1945

How bitter it is when the world's jubilation is for the defeat, the deepest humiliation of one's own country. This shows yet again how terrible the abyss is, that has opened between Germany, the land of our fathers and masters, and the civilized world."

(Heinrich Mann, 10 May 1945)

to him behind … For every hour we keep fighting, the terrible suffering of the civilian population of Berlin and our injured soldiers will be prolonged. Therefore, in agreement with the high command of the Soviet forces I ask you to stop fighting immediately."

When the last Wehrmacht and SS units surrendered on 2 May 1945, the battle for the Reich capital ended – Berlin had capitulated.

„Hurrah, we're still alive!"
Berliners shouted. But for many of the surviving civilians in the destroyed city the struggle continued. Presumably more than 110 000 women were raped by Soviet soldiers.

It had not been forgotten, what german troops had done during the assault of the Soviet Union, killing about 30 Million people, men, women, children and even babies. Nonetheless the Soviet

Administration immediately took over the organisation of food supply for the Berliners and organized the first clearing up measures, but the division of Berlin was already on the cards of the former allies. In July 1945, French, British and US-Troops came to Berlin and seized their respective occupational districts in the western parts of Berlin, while the Soviet Administration remained in the central and eastern part of the city.

Reminders of the Battle for Berlin:
▷ Reichstag (Parliament)
▷ Soviet War Memorials Tiergarten, Treptow, Schönholzer Heide
▷ „Scars of Remembrance"
▷ Airraid Shelters Friedrichshain, Humboldthain
▷ Allied Museum
▷ Memorial Seelow Heights
▷ „Führer Bunker"

Red Army soldiers restage the raising of the Soviet flag on the Reichstag.

1 Military parade for Hitler's 50th birthday, 20 April 1939, view from the Victory Column to the Brandenburg Gate

INNER CITY DISTRICTS Numerous traces of „National Socialist" history can still be found outside the former government district. How many people know that the Victory Column was used as radio control station for German planes during the „Battle of Berlin", while the „Straße des 17. Juni" served as a runway? Or who still knows about Madam Kitty's, the espionage brothel of the SS? Or the Heavy Load Testing Body with a weight of 12 360 tons, one of the last remnants of the plans for „Germania", capital of the world? Another little known fact is that Konrad Zuse built the first computer ever on Kreuzberg Heights in 1941. Only a small plaque marks the site, which saw, in the middle of the war, the beginning of a new age.

1
Victory Column, Great Star, Straße des 17. Juni
⌂ Heinrich Strack, 1873/Albert Speer, 1938 → Straße des 17. Juni, Map B2
Ⓢ Bellevue ⏰ Mon, Sun 8.00–22.00
The first step in the realization of the plans to transform Berlin into the ▷ world metropolis „Germania" was the remodeling of the „east-west axis". Albert Speer had the „Großer Stern Square" extended from 80 to 200 meters and moved the Victory Column from its traditional place in front of the ▷ Reichstag to the Großer Stern in 1938. At that time the monument had three segments, commemorating the Prussian victories over Denmark, Austria and France. On Hitler's explicit orders, a fourth segment was added – for a war still to be won? Along the circled square were placed the monuments of the Chancellor Bismarck, General Field Marshal Moltke and War Minister Roon. Today you can still enter the traffic island safely via tunnels starting in Speer's pavilions. Along the finished „east-west axis" Hitler demonstrated his military power in a five-hour Wehrmacht parade in 1939. Only a few years later however, parts of the boulevard had to be covered with camouflage nets, to disorient Allied

bombers. In the last days of the war, the Victory Column was used as a radio control station for German fighter and transport planes, such as the Ju 52, which landed and took off on Charlottenburger Chaussee (Straße des 17. Juni), to bring supplies to the encircled city. The Victory Column was not very popular with the French occupying forces; in 1946 they demanded to blow it up. In the end, only the reliefs at the base were taken to France as war trophies and later returned to Berlin for the 750-year celebrations in 1987.

2
Street Lights
⌂ Albert Speer, 1938 → Bismarckstraße, Map B2 Ⓢ Tiergarten
Lighting the new „east-west axis" proved to be a particular problem. The vista was not to be interrupted by streetlights hanging above the street. Albert Speer finally developed a design which was introduced to Hitler in the garden of the ▷ New Reich Chancellery and which met with his approval. Towards the end of the war all lanterns between the underground station Tiergarten and the ▷ Brandenburg Gate were dismantled to create a runway for planes. Of the originally 703 candelabra about half have survived.

Hermann Göring 1893–1946

As one of the most successful pilots of the First World War, Göring received the highest German order, the „**Pour le Mérite**" and was given the command of the fighter squadron No 1 „Freiherr von Richthofen". In 1921 he met Hitler, joined the NSDAP and became temporarily chief of the SA. After his election as President of the Reichstag in 1932, he managed to gain further positions. He was made Prussian Minister of the Interior in 1933, Reich Minister of Aviation, Reich Forestry and Reich Hunting Master. Together with Himmler and Heydrich he was instrumental in setting up the reign of terror and established the first concentration camps.

3
Tax Office Charlottenburg

Brucker/Kepler, 1936–1939 → Bismarckstraße 48, Map A2 Bismarckstraße On Allied orders all Nazi emblems in post-war Germany had to be removed. Above the gate of the Charlottenburg tax office, built in 1939, as above other entrances in Germany, a relic of the „Third Reich" remained.
The Reich eagle, designed by Kurt Schmidt-Ehmen, no longer holds the swastika in its stone talons but a sign with the house number.

4
Zoo Flak Tower

Friedrich Tamms, 1941 → Zoologischer Garten, Map B3 Zoologischer Garten In 1940 Hitler commissioned one of the largest building projects in the history of mankind: 200 million cubic meters of concrete were to be fused into air-raid shelters all over Germany. He gave instructions to erect six anti-aircraft towers in Berlin's inner city parks. Three were actually completed before the end of the war: **Zoo Flak Tower**, ▷ **Flak Towers Humboldthain** and **Friedrichshain**.
The first one to be built was Zooshelter in 1941. Friedrich Tamms, who went on to build similar Anti Aircraft towers in Vienna and Hamburg, took over as project director from Albert Speer. The castle-like structure of reinforced concrete measured 70.5 by 70.5 meters, with a height of 42 m and walls of up to 2.5 m thick. On the roof platform stood four twin anti aircraft guns (12.8 cm), controlled by a smaller command bunker, with a maximum range of 14 800 meters in height. Self-sufficient through its own supply of water and electricity, 22 000 people found shelter from the bombs. Also art treasures from the Berlin museums, such as the bust of **Nofretete**, now to be admired in on the Museum Isle, were hidden here. The command bunker itself provided shelter for another 8 000 people.
In 1946 a British demolition squad failed to blow up the bunker, which had survived the war more or less intact. Only in 1948 was complete demolition achieved.

5
Embassy of Spain

Johannes & Walter Krüger, 1938–1943 → Lichtensteinallee 1, Map B3 Zoologischer Garten The Inspector General for Buildings Office under Albert Speer was responsible for the realization of this project. The Krüger brothers previously had planned the Tannenberg Memorial in Eastern Prussia (1924–1926). While the fascist regime of General Franco was not Germany's direct ally, the monumental building shows many affinities between the two states. After war dam-

As Commander-in-Chief of the Luftwaffe he was responsible for the deployment of the **Condor Legion** during the civil war in Spain, and, with his appointment as general field marshal in 1938, he became the most powerful man after Hitler.

In 1940 he was awarded the specifically created title „Reich Marshal of the Great German Reich". After losing the

Battle of Britain and the defeat at Stalingrad, his influence began to wane. A morphine addict, he began to withdraw from the public and spent more time in his private refuge, the palatial estate ▷ „**Carinhall**", north of Berlin. On 8 May 1945 he was taken prisoner by US authorities and condemned to death at the Nuremberg trials. Some hours before his execution he committed suicide by taking cyanide. His diamond-studded Marshal's staff is displayed, together with Hitler's golden pistol, in the museum of the Military Academy at West Point, New York, USA.

Göring claimed if enemy airplanes were ever to enter German airspace, people could call him Meyer. Only a few years later many German towns lay in ruins.

---

age had been removed together with the fascist emblems over the portico, the embassy was reopened in 2003.

6
Embassy of Yugoslavia / German Council on Foreign Relations
⌂ Werner March, 1938–1940
→ Rauchstraße 17–18. Map B3
Ⓢ Ⓤ Zoologischer Garten The former embassy of Yugoslavia was designed by Werner March, the architect of the Olympic Stadium, as a villa with two wings and façade decoration by Arno Breker. After Germany's attack on Yugoslavia in 1941, it was used as a guest-house, and temporarily was the seat of the Minister of Occupied Eastern Regions. Since 1953 it was the office of the Claims Court set up by the Allies, which dealt with compensation claims of victims of the Nazi dictatorship. Today it houses the German Council on Foreign Relations.

7
Kaiser Wilhelm Memorial Church
⌂ Franz Schwechten, 1895 → Breit-scheidplatz. Map B3 Ⓢ Ⓤ Zoologischer Garten The ruins of the Kaiser Wilhelm Memorial Church were left untouched as a war memorial and were the landmark of West Berlin during the partition. After taking down part of the church in the 1950s, Egon Eiermann added a tower and the nave.

Inside is kept the „**Cross of Coventry**" to remind of the devastating bombing raid on the British city by the Nazi Luftwaffe (Airforce).

8
Bureau IV B4 of the Reich Security Central Office
⌂ Karl Bernhard, 1910 → Kurfürstenstraße 115/116. Map B3 Ⓤ Wittenbergplatz The Bureau IV B4 was SS-Obersturmbannführer Adolf Eichmann's office since 1939. As head of the „**Reich Central Office for Jewish Emigration and Relocation**" he was responsible for the deportation of millions of Jews into concentration and extermination camps, as part of the so-called „**final solution**

7

21 Jewish Museum

16 Emblem of the Reich Railways

21 Garden of Exile in the Jewish Museum

8 Memorial site at Adolf Eichmann's former central office

5 Spanish Embassy

1 Victory Column

12 Contemporary relief at Fehrbelliner Platz

of the Jewish question", agreed at the Wannsee conference on 20 January 1942 by SS and ministry officials. Here he organized the transport of Jews from all over Europe to the SS-death camps. In 1946 Eichmann managed to escape from American custody and fled to Argentina, where he worked under a false name for Mercedes-Benz Argentina.

He was discovered by agents of the Israeli secret service Mossad in 1960, smuggled to Israel, put on trial and condemned to death.

The Berlin building was demolished in 1961, and today plaques in the bus shelter of line 100 recall this site of German history.

9
Jewish Community Center
⌂ Dieter Knoblauch, Heinz Heise, 1959
→ Fasanenstraße 79–80, Map B3
Ⓢ Ⓤ Zoologischer Garten
No more than three percent of the 160 000 Jewish citizens of Berlin managed to survive hidden in the city. The others were either forced to leave or sent to concentration camps.
Heavily damaged during the November pogrom in 1938, the synagogue in Fasanenstraße was dismantled in 1957 and parts of the facade were used for the new building.
Today, the Jewish community in Berlin is again the largest in Germany (11 000 members).

10
Heinrich Mann's Apartment
→ Fasanenstraße 61, Map B3
Ⓢ Ⓤ Zoologischer Garten
After the First World War, Heinrich Mann praised Berlin as a **"school for democracy"** and was head of the poets' section of the Academy of Arts, to which his brother Thomas Mann also belonged. He lived in this house until 1933. After Hitler became Chancellor, the Manns were forced into exile by the Nazis and fled via France to the USA. Shortly after his 1950 nomination as president of the Academy of Arts of the GDR Heinrich Mann died in Santa

Monica, California. He was buried in the Dorotheenstadt Cemetery on Chaussee-straße in the Berlin city district „Mitte".

11
Madam Kitty's
→ Giesebrechtstraße 11, Map A3
Ⓤ Adenauerplatz Kitty Schmidt's luxu-riously decorated salon-brothel was the meeting point for diplomats, ambas-sadors and high-ranking members of Berlin society.
In 1939, following orders from Reinhard Heydrich and under the direction of the Foreign Security Service head Walter Schellenberg, **„Operation Kitty"** trans-formed the brothel into an espionage center. Every room was bugged, double walls were inserted, and a monitoring center was installed in the cellar, re-cording all conversations and events on tape.
Female staff were recruited from all over Europe and trained by the security service to gain secret information from the guests while in the throes of sexual passion.
The Italian ambassador is said to have made negative utterances about Hitler, leading to a final deterioration of rela-tions with Italy.
By 1943, when „Operation Kitty" was ended, about 25 000 tapes had been collected; but at the end of the war they disappeared from the Gestapo archives. The former brothel rooms were converted into apartments.

Fehrbelliner Square
⌂ Otto Fierle, 1935, Map A4 Ⓤ Fehr-belliner Platz As part of a competition to redesign Fehrbelliner Square, Otto Fierle's design of half-circles was the winner, and by 1943 four office blocks were finished.
Today's town hall of Wilmersdorf was first used by the Wehrmacht and after the war as the British headquarters, named „Lancaster House".
As a gift, the former occupying force left a shining red London telephone box next to the entrance. In the building next door the Film Stock of the Federal Archives of Germany is kept.

Joseph Goebbels 1897–1945

Goebbels was born in Rheydt near Mönchengladbach to working class parents. After a childhood illness he was left with a crippled foot. He completed his doctorate in Heidelberg and since signed with the abbreviation „Dr. G.". He failed to secure a job as a journalist, being refused by numerous Jewish publishing firms. He joined the NSDAP and was appointed Gauleiter (regional leader) for Berlin by Hitler in 1926. Since 1933 he was „Minister for Public Enlightenment and Propaganda", a newly founded ministry to perfectionate the propaganda pouring down on Germany. He created the „cult of the Führer" around Hitler, intensified anti-Semitism through films such as „Jew Süß" and „The Eternal Jew" and personally organized the November pogrom in 1938. After the defeat at Stalingrad he held his infamous speech in the ▷ „Sportpalast", calling for „total war". In 1945, when the Soviet troops were already advancing on Berlin, he continued to talk of the „final victory" and ▷ „miracle weapons" which would turn the tide in Germany's favour. On 22 April 1945 he and his family joined Hitler in the ▷ „Führer Bunker" to be at Hitler's side. After Hitler's suicide he was named his successor. Only a few hours later after having poisoned their six children he committed suicide together with his wife Magda.

The people's radio set was named „Volksempfänger 301" after 30 January, the day of Hitler's appointment as Chancellor. It cost only 35 Reichsmark in 1938. Nick-

named „Goebbel's snout", it provided the means for Goebbels to reach about 65 percent of all German households by 1941.

13
Erich Kästner's Apartment
→ Prager Straße 6, Map B3

Ⓤ Spichernstraße The writer, journalist and scriptwriter Erich Kästner was one of the most successful literary talents in pre-Nazi Germany. Famous for his poems, essays and novels for children and adults and outspoken enemy of the Nazis, he was inhibited from publishing in Germany after 1933.

When on 10 May 1933 his books were burnt on Opera Square (today Bebel Square) under the slogan „**Against decadence and moral decay. For order and decency in family and state**", Kästner was an eye witness in the crowd. Arrested several times by the Gestapo, he always managed to get free. Kästner did not emigrate, published his books under a pseudonym and wrote, among others, the script for the film „Münchhausen". A plaque indicates where the house he used to live in, destroyed in the war, once was.

14
Marlene Dietrich's Apartment
→ Bundesallee 54, Map B4

Ⓢ Ⓤ Bundesplatz Marlene Dietrich was born in Schöneberg, Leberstraße 65. Around 1925 the then unknown actress moved with husband and daughter into an elegant flat on the top floor of what is today Bundesallee. Following the success of the film „The Blue Angel" she went to Hollywood in 1930 and signed a seven-year contract with Paramount Pictures. Goebbels offered her 200 000 Reichsmarks for every film she were to make in Germany, choosing her own script, director and producer. She refused and from 1943 supported the American troops with 500 personal appearances in a front theatre show in their fight against the Nazi regime.

On 6 May 1992 she died in Paris and was buried according to her last will in the Friedenau cemetery in Berlin. Some „incorrigibles" protested against this, accusing her of treason to her country during the war.

15
Palace of Sports
⌂ Hermann Dernburg, 1910 → Potsdamer Straße Ecke Pallasstraße, Map C3 Ⓤ Kleistpark During the Weimar Republic nearly all political parties staged major events here. The Nazi party declared the Palace of Sports later the „home of the movement".
Here, on 18 February 1943, after the lost Battle of Stalingrad, Propaganda Minister Joseph Goebbels held his speech on **„total war"**.
In an attempt to restore people's faith in the **„final victory"** he asked the crowd of 15 000 frenzied followers **„Do you want total war? A war more total and more radical than we can possibly imagine today?"** The answer was unanonimously **„yes!"**.
The hall was completely destroyed by air raids in 1944. Today, in its place there is a housing complex.

16
Reich Railways Central Office
⌂ Armin Wegener, 1895 → Schöneberger Ufer 1–3, Map C3 Ⓤ Gleisdreieck On the back of the building, overlooking the elevated railway, is a projection with the stone emblem of the former German Reich Railways: eagle wings on a wheel. The swastika relief underneath was removed after the war.

17
Heavy Load Testing Body
⌂ Albert Speer, 1941 → General-Pape-Straße 2, Map C4 Ⓢ Papestraße According to Hitler's vision, here on the north-south axis of the ▷ **world metropolis „Germania"** was to be erected a gigantic ▷ **Arch of Triumph** for the German soldiers killed in the First World War. With its height of 117 meters and 170 meters width, the smaller Arc de Triomphe in Paris would have fitted nearly 9 times in its Berlin counterpart. In order to test how the sandy soil would withstand the pressure of its weight, the Inspector General for Buildings had French slave laborers erect a 12 360-ton concrete cylinder. The colossus is 21 meters in diameter, 14 meters above and 18 meters underground.
The engineers noted a settlement of 19 cm: the building of the Arch would thus have been possible. While contracts with Swedish granite companies had already been signed, the actual construction work was never begun due to the begin of the war. The oldest and largest Heavy Load Testing Body in the world is under preservation order and one of the few silent witnesses to the „Germania" designs. The Body stands in the northeast angle of the planned ▷ **Arch of Triumph**.

17 Heavy load testing body

Nazi Propaganda

During the Weimar Republic, the Nazi party were already using the means of propaganda more intensively than any other party, pointing out the „national dishonor" of the Versailles Peace treaty, signed by Germany at the end of the First World War. The Nazis also singled out Jews, communists and democrats as enemies of the state. The stylizing of Hitler as the bringer of salvation, and the party rallies, carefully choreographed down to the smallest detail, all contributed to the fascination Hitler had for the masses. **„Hitler all over Germany"** was the slogan for Hitler's election campaign flights in 1932. He managed to visit three towns per day and to appear omnipresent in Germany. After he came to power, the newly founded ▷ **ministry for public enlightenment and propaganda** influenced all areas of life in Germany. With the start of the war, military propaganda took over. Generals were feted as idols, and campaigns such as **„The enemy listens too"** were to familiarize the people with the correct behaviour in wartime. Even when the end was close, a senseless final attempt was made to appeal to the population's will to hold out for the „final victory".

Ludwig Hohlwein's recruitment poster „And You?" (1932) is now part of the collection of the Museum of Modern Art in New York.

UND DU?

18
Konrad Zuse's House
→ Methfesselstraße 7, Map D4 Ⓤ Platz der Luftbrücke At this site, in 1941, the engineer Konrad Zuse developed the „Z3", the first fully functioning computer in the world. As early as 1936, Zuse had developed the idea of a program-controlled computing machine, which resulted in the „Z1" in 1938. Zuse was deemed indispensable to the war effort and was thus able to found his company **„Zuse Ingenieurbüro und Apparatebau, Berlin"**. He repeatedly tried to convince the Army Ordnance Office of the usefulness of his invention by presenting it to the ▷ **German Research Institute for Aviation**, but was met primarily by incomprehension. The Z-computers and the workshop were destroyed in a bombing raid in 1945. Before his company was amalgamated into the Siemens Corporation in 1967, Zuse built 251 computers in total. A replica of the „Z1" can be found in the „Deutsches Technik-Museum Berlin" (German Technical Museum) on Trebbiner Straße 66, close to Potsdamer Platz.

19
Tempelhof Airfield
⌂ Ernst Sagebiel, 1935–1941 → Platz der Luftbrücke 1–6, Map D4 Ⓤ Platz der Luftbrücke While the „World Airfield Tempelhof" was being constructed, plans for its closure already existed. The future capital **„Germania"** was to have four airports on the outskirts of the city. Even today the „gigantic clothes hanger" with a length of 1230 meters is one of the largest interconnected building complexes in Europe. The roof construction, extending 40 m over the forecourt, was designed as a spectator terrace for air displays and was to provide space for 90 000 spectators. Towards the end of the war, fighter planes were being constructed for Junkers and Focke-Wulf on an assembly line underneath the departure and arrival halls and taken straight onto the runway. The Memorial to the Berlin Airlift (Luftbrückendenkmal) with its three spikes facing west recalls the

three Allied air corridors during the Soviet blockade in 1948/49. Up to 1962 a Reich eagle sat 45 m high on the roof of the reception area. It was then presented to the Americans for their military museum at West Point (New York). When leaving Berlin, the Air Force presented the head of the statue to the city of Berlin. It now stands on Eagle Square in front of the airfield reception building.

German-Jewish history is impressively displayed and documented here.

20
Columbiahouse
Concentration Camp

⌂ 1933 → Columbiadamm 1–3, Map D4 Ⓤ Platz der Luftbrücke Up to 1936, the Tempelhofer Feld prison was situated here. After 1933, it was used by the SS and the Gestapo as a prison for 8 000 political prisoners. It was a so-called „wild camp" and used as a „training camp" for concentration camp commanders and personnel, where they learned how to torture. In 1936 it was pulled down to make way for the new ▷**Tempelhof Airfield**. Today, a steel sculpture at Columbiadamm and Golssener Straße commemorates the prison.

21
Jewish Museum of Berlin

⌂ Daniel Libeskind, 2001 → Lindenstraße 9–14, Map D3 Ⓤ Kochstraße ⏱ Mon–Sun 10–20 Built by the famous American architect Daniel Libeskind, this is one of the most spectacular new buildings in Berlin. The zigzag ground plan recalls an exploded Star of David, scar-like fissures represent the sufferings of the German Jews.

22
Printing Workshop of the German Labour Front/ Metal Workers' Union

⌂ Mendelsohn, Reichel, 1930 → Alte Jacobstraße 148/149, Map D3 Ⓤ Hallesches Tor After the abolition of the unions in 1933, this building was used by the Deutsche Arbeitsfront (German Labour Front). Dutch conscripted laborers produced commercial printed goods and Nazi literature. For foreign workers, magazines in 20 different languages were printed. Today the complex again is property of the Print Workers Union.

23
Central Office for Jews

→ Fontanepromenade 15, Map D4 Ⓤ Südstern After the pogroms of 9 November 1938, this office was separated from the State Employment Center to administer the allocation of labour of the Berlin Jews. All men between 18 and 55 and women up to 50 were registered and assigned hard labour in the so-called „Jewish crews". During the **„Operation Factory"** in February 1943, all Jews were taken from their place of work and deported to concentration camps.

24
Gasometer Shelter

⌂ Baustab Wilhelmi under the Inspector General for Buildings Albert Speer, 1942 → Fichtestraße 4–12, Map E4 Ⓤ Südstern As part of the **bunker-building program for the Reich capital**, a bunker was constructed inside the gasometer of the „British Imperial Continental Gas Association", built by Eugen Reissner in 1826.

Up to 30 000 people found shelter in 770 windowless rooms on six levels, behind walls of 1.8 m thickness and a top ceiling of 3 meter thick concrete. After the war, the shelter was used until well into the 1950s to house refugees from the east, as a youth prison and for food storage. Today, the building is empty.

25
Armaments Factory Ernst Franke

→ Admiralstraße 17, Map E3

Ⓤ Kottbusser Tor Just one of the numerous companies using conscripted labour forces of about 400 000 women and men, this former munitions factory represents the exploitation of European „foreign workers" during the „Third Reich". Metal parts for hand guns, bombs, assault guns and armored vehicles were produced here.

About 50 Soviet forced laborers had to work under such inhumane conditions that the owner was widely known as „slave-driver Franke". Ten of the labourers were kept in the former boiler room in the second courtyard, still standing today.

26
Soviet War Memorial Treptow

⌂ Yakov Belopolski, 1949 → Treptower Park, Map F4 Ⓢ Treptower Park Replacing a simple memorial stone, the greatest Soviet Memorial in Berlin was built in 1946 as a „symbol of the victory of the glorious Soviet Army over Hitler fascism".

The center of the memorial, built from granite from the demolished ▷ **New Reich Chancellery**, is the bronze sculpture, 13 meters high, of a Red Army soldier, his sword on the shattered swastika and a German child in his arms. More than 5 000 Soviet soldiers found their final resting place here.

27
Underground Shelter

⌂ Baustab Wilhelmi under the Inspector General for Buildings Albert Speer, 1942 → Klosterstraße, Map E2 Ⓤ Klosterstraße As early as 1937 the Nazis thought about using the Berlin underground railway network as air-raid shelters in case of a military conflict. During the „**shelter building program for the Reich capital**", an air-raid shelter was built into the shell of the future underground station Klosterstraße, with 150 rooms. During GDR times, the bunker was used to cultivate mushrooms. Today, for particular occasions, the shelter is open to visitors.

28
Flak Towers Friedrichshain & Humboldthain

⌂ Friedrich Tamms, 1942 → Volkspark Friedrichshain & Humboldthain, Map E2, D1 Ⓤ Strausberger Platz, Ⓢ Ⓤ Gesundbrunnen The Flak Tower in Friedrichshain, of the same construction as the ▷ **Zoo Flak Tower**, was blown up after the war, splitting it in two halves. It was then covered in rubble. Of the Flak Tower Humboldthain, erected close to the ▷ **AEG factory**, only the southern part and the smaller command bunker could be demolished and were also filled up with rubble. Today, from the 42 m high platforms on the north side, you have a good view over Berlin. The Berlin Underworld Association (Berliner-Unterwelten-Verein) will take visitors inside the tower.

29
Regional Office of the Nazi party in the District of Berlin

⌂ Walther & Johannes Krüger, 1938 → Am Friedrichshain 22, Map F2 Ⓢ Ⓤ Alexanderplatz On the 5 January 1919 the German Workers' Party (Deutsche Arbeiterpartei – DAP) was founded in Munich and renamed the following year as National Socialist German Workers' Party (Nationalsozialistische Deutsche Arbeiterpartei – NSDAP). Repeatedly banned because of its radicalism and

19 Head of the Reich eagle at „Eagle Square"

27 Light well in the shelter

27 Buildingplan in the shelter

27 Gas lock in subway shelter

28 Flak Tower Humboldthain

26 Lenin and Red Army soldiers in Reich Chancellery granite

26 Detail at the portal of the Memorial

26 Soviet War Memorial in Treptow

| Old Germans | First Empire | German Federation | Second Empire |
| 500 | 800 | 1848 | 1871 |

The German Eagle

The German coat of arms, the black eagle on a golden shield, is the oldest European national emblem still in use. Its origins can be traced back to the Germanic tribes, who revered the eagle as a symbol of the sun, strength and the highest god. From 1200 onwards, the red eagle was generally acknowledged as the emblem of the German people. Over the centuries, the eagle design was changed many times. Hitler turned the emblem of the Nazi party, his own design based on the eagle of the Roman legions, into the emblem of the „Third Reich". In its current form the eagle is the national symbol of the reunited Germany.

the failed beer hall putsch of 1923, it was still able to establish itself in and beyond Bavaria. During his imprisonment Hitler formulated the strategic concept for the years to come: **„Instead of trying to gain power through force of arms, we will stick our noses into the Reichstag, much to the annoyance of the Catholic and Marxist members of parliament. It might take longer to outvote them rather than to outshoot them, but in the end, their own constitution will guarantee our success."** To establish a foothold in „red Berlin" where the party had only 500 members in 1926, Hitler appointed Joseph Goebbels as Gauleiter of Berlin-Brandenburg. After the erection of the New Reich Chancellery at Voss-Street, where also the regional seat of the Nazi

party had been, a new office complex was planned here in the midst of former workers district „Prenzlauer Berg". After the war, the eagle and swastika in the gable and the sculptures on both sides of the entry gates were removed. Today the building is the home of a publishing company.

30
Air-raid Shelter Gesundbrunnen
⌂ Baustab Wilhelmi under the Inspector General for Buildings Albert Speer, 1938 → U-Bahnhof Gesundbrunnen, Map D1 Ⓢ Ⓤ Gesundbrunnen, ⏲ Sat 12–18 The deepest of all underground stations in Berlin was changed into an air-raid shelter in 1938, protecting up to 4 000 people from the bomb-

State Employment Office Berlin-Brandenburg

Olympic Area

German Post

Tax Office Charlottenburg

Weimar Republic
1922

„Third Reich"
1935

FRG
1975

Germany
1995

ing raids. The Berlin Underworld Association (Berliner-Unterwelten-Verein) opens up the bunker for visitors at weekends.

31
AEG Plant Humboldthain
⌂ Peter Behrens, 1895 → Gustav-Meyer-Allee 25, Map D1 Ⓢ Ⓤ Gesundbrunnen In 1892 the electrical company Allgemeine Elektrizitätsgesellschaft (AEG) established one of the most important industrial sites in Berlin. Competing with Siemens for the construction of an **underground traffic system**, the first tunnel train in Berlin was built underneath the plant in 1897 as a testing range. The contract went to Siemens, nonetheless. Used as an air-raid shelter during the Second World War, the tunnel can be visited at certain times. AEG emerged from the German Edison Society in 1883 and was dissolved in 1996. The building ensemble around the 203-meter long turbine house is one of the icons of early industrial design and is being used by various companies as well as the Technical University of Berlin. A plaque at the main entrance commemorates the Polish conscripted laborers working here for the AEG during the Nazi dictatorship.

32
Invaliden Cemetery
⌂ 1748 → Scharnhorststraße 25, Map C2 Ⓢ Ⓤ Hauptbahnhof/Lehrter Bahnhof The Invaliden Cemetery is one of Berlin's oldest cemeteries and a national monument. In close proximity to the government district it demonstrates in impressive fashion the fleeting nature of military power. General Fieldmarshal Helmuth von Moltke, Alfred von Schlieffen, the head of the ▷ „**Organisation Todt**" Fritz Todt, as well as combat pilots such as the „Red Baron" Manfred von Richthofen, Ernst Udet and Werner Mölders are buried here. The grave of SS-Obergruppenführer Reinhard Heydrich, who was assassinated in Prague in 1942, was obliterated after the war. With the building of the Berlin Wall in 1961, the cemetery became part of the border area, and was heavily damaged by the fortification measures of the GDR military. Many of the 3 000 graves were demolished.

Invaliden Cemetery

Tempelhof Airfield

Steglitz Post Office

Olympic bell

32 Sleeping lion on Scharnhorst's tomb

32 Invaliden Cemetery

32 Tomb of Colonel General von Seeckt

32 Tomb von Schlieffen Family

34 Exhibition room at the Plötzensee Memorial

34 Execution shed at Plötzensee

35 Barracks on „Speer-Plate"

34 Urn with soil from concentration camps

33
Freight Station Putlitzbrücke
→ Map B1 Ⓢ Westhafen The majority
of the 50 000 Berlin Jews were deported to the SS-concentration camps in
Germany and eastern europe from this
freight station.
This is commemorated by a memorial
at the S-Bahnhof.

34
Plötzensee Prison /
Plötzensee Memorial
⌂ Bruno Grimmek, 1952 → Hüttig-
pfad, Map A1 Ⓢ Beusselstraße
🕐 Mon – Sun 9 – 17 The Plötzensee
prison was originally built in 1879.
Under the Nazi regime, between 1933
and 1945, about 3 000 opponents of
the regime were executed here.
Among them are the conspirators of the
20 July 1944 assassination attempt on
Hitler, members of the Kreisau Circle
and many non-German prisoners. The
Plötzensee Memorial was installed here
in 1951.

35
„Speer Plate"
⌂ Carl Christoph Lörcher, 1942
→ Friedrich-Olbricht-Damm 63 – 73,
Map A1 Ⓢ Beusselstraße The concret-
ed-over open space of 10 hectares,
the so-called „Speer-Plate", was part of
the barracks complex of the ▷„Organisation Todt".
Set up especially for the planned transformation of Berlin, the „Transport Unit
Speer" of the National Socialist Motor
Corps (NSKK) was stationed here, using
the „Speer-Plate" as parking space for
their fleet of motor vehicles.
It was planned to use the space to
store the granite slabs needed for the
▷Great Hall. In the bunker „Plötzensee-
plan", disguised as a house, Inspector
General for Building Albert Speer stored
all documents relating to the transformation of Berlin.
Since 1955 the space was used as coal
storage for West Berlin. Today a home
improvement store is situated on the
site. Some of the barracks were pulled
down in 2000.

The Iron Cross
Ever since gold was exchanged for iron
during the war against Napoleon, under
the slogan **„Gold I gave for iron"**, cast
iron was considered a patriotic metal –
what better material was there for military
decorations? In 1813 King Friedrich
Wilhelm IV. created the Iron Cross, designed by Karl Friedrich von Schinkel,
with three grades, Second and First Class
and the Grand Cross. With the start of
the Second World War, the swastika sup-
planted the king's monogram and the
crown in the middle. Adolf Hitler, himself
holder the Iron Cross Second and First
Class, added the Knight's Cross, which
was up-graded four times during the
war. The only person to be awarded the
Knight's Cross with golden oak leaves
and swords and diamonds, was pilot
Colonel Rudel. According to westgerman
law, passed on 26 July 1957, the Iron
Cross may be worn publicly once the
swastika has been removed.

Top: The Iron Cross Second Class
of 1939

1 „Victory" by Arno Breker (1936) at the House of German Sports

OUTER DISTRICTS & BRANDENBURG Outside the city center and on the outskirts of Berlin numerous relics from the city's darkest era can still be found. The party grandees of the Nazi regime resided in villas confiscated from their Jewish owners or had luxurious hunting lodges built in the Schorfheide (scurf heath, a forest district north of Berlin), like Hermann Göring and Joseph Goebbels. In the Berlin quarter of Dahlem, at the „Kaiser-Wilhelm-Institut für Physik", Werner Heisenberg conducted research on the German atom bomb, while in Kummersdorf Wernher von Braun built and tested the first rockets. Beyond the city gates, the Sachsenhausen concentration camp represents of one of the grimmest chapters in the history of Berlin and is a forceful reminder of the past.

Reich Sporting Field

1

Reich Sporting Field, Olympic Grounds and Olympic Stadium
⌂ Werner March, 1936
→ Olympischer Platz, Map B3
Ⓢ Ⓤ Olympiastadion

On 13 May 1931, Berlin was chosen to host the Summer Olympic Games of 1936.

The Nazi regime was quick to seize this opportunity to gain enormous prestige, nationally and internationally. The development of the Reichssportfeld became, together with the Nuremberg party rally grounds, the most important building project of the Nazis.

On 1 August 1936 Hitler opened the XI Olympic Games from the „Führer's balcony", recently restored to its original state. For a few weeks, the world was taken in by the dazzling show. The French athletes even greeted Hitler with the „German salute".

At 25 television points, established all over Berlin, people were able to watch live what was happening a few miles away. All anti-Semitic slogans had vanished overnight, and the media were ordered to discontinue their persecution of the Jews for the duration of the games.

Yet only 35 km north of the Olympic Grounds, prisoners were toiling to erect the ▷ **Sachsenhausen concentration camp**. Jesse Owen's becoming the spectators' favorite athlete was something the regime could not prevent. Hitler refused to shake the African-American's hand and left the stadium. In 2006, the Berlin Olympic stadium will host the final of the soccer World Cup.

May Field and Bell Tower
⌂ Werner March, 1936 → Am Glockenturm, Map B3 Ⓢ Ⓤ Olympiastadion ⏱ Apr–Nov 9–18

The Maifeld (may field), intended for mass events, could accommodate up to 400 000 participants and spectators. It is framed by the western wall and in its center a bell tower rises up 76 m.

In its base is the Langemarck Hall, established in honor of the 2 000 volunteer recruits who on 10 November 1914, as the story goes, charged the enemy singing the German national anthem and were all shot down.

After the Second World War the damaged tower had to be demolished, but was rebuilt in 1962, with a viewing platform at the top.

The damaged Olympic Bell was recast, according to Werner March's design. The original is now in front of the nearby ▷ **House of German Sports**.

1 Water Buffalo in front of the House of German Sports

REICH SPORTING FIELD 1936

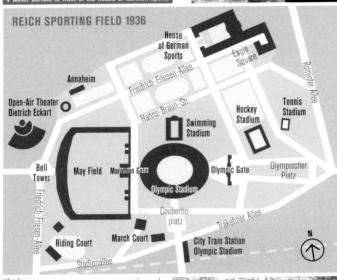

House of German Sports

Eagle Square

Rominter Allee

Annaheim

Friedrich-Friesen-Allee

Open-Air Theater Dietrich Eckart

Hanns-Braun-Str.

Hockey Stadium

Tennis Stadium

Swimming Stadium

Bell Tower

May Field

Marathon Gate

Olympic Gate

Olympischer Platz

Friedrich-Friesen-Allee

Olympic Stadium

Coubertin-platz

Trakehner Allee

N

Riding Court

March Court

City Train Station Olympic Stadium

Stadionallee

1 May Field and Olympic Stadium, 2001

1 Detail of the Olympic bell

BERLIN·1936
1.-16. AUG
OLYMPISCHE SPIELE

Berlin ruft zur Olympiade

Alternative design by John Heartfield, 1936

Open-Air Theater
Dietrich Eckart/Forest Stage
⌂ Werner March, 1936 → Am Glockenturm, Map B3 Ⓢ Ⓤ Olympiastadion

The open-air theatre at the end of Murellenschlucht, named after the Nazi poet Eckart, was built for an audience of 20 000 and designed to recall ancient amphitheaters.

In the woods to the west, a row of mirrors is engraved with quotations by the victims of Nazi justice shot and killed here at Murellenberg.

House of German Sports
⌂ Werner March, 1936 → Friedrich-Friesen-Allee, Map B3 Ⓢ Ⓤ Olympiastadion ⊙ Wed–Sun 10–18

After the war the British forces headquarters in Berlin moved into this building, originally built to house athletes. Today the athletes are back, and a museum documents the history of the Reichssportfeld.

One of the exhibits is the original Olympic Bell of 1936 at the main entrance. Engraved are the Brandenburg Gate, the Reich eagle with the Olympic rings in its talons, slightly abraded swastikas and the words **„11th Olympic Games Berlin"** and **„I call upon the youth of the world"**.

The bullet hole came from a German Anti Aircraft gunner, who unintentionally hit the bell in the nearby tower during practice.

2
Reich Court Martial
⌂ Heinrich Keyser, Karl von Großheim, 1910 → Witzlebenstraße 4–10, Map B3 Ⓤ Sophie-Charlotte-Platz

In the Reich Court Martial, the highest authority of Wehrmacht jurisdiction, between 1936 and 1945 more than 260 conscientious objectors and numerous members of the resistance were sentenced to death for of their stance against the Nazi regime.

3
Central Office of the Reich Labour Service
⌂ Kurt Heinrich Tischler, 1938 → Bismarckplatz 1, Map B3 Ⓢ Halensee

The central office of the Reichsarbeitsdienst was designed as an office block with 400 rooms. From 1935, all men between 18 and 25 were recruited for a six-month period of labor service. Under the slogan **„With spade and grain"**, work brigades marched through Germany helping to build autobahns and the West Wall. By 1939, about 350 000 men had performed this **„service of honor for the German people"**. With the beginning of the war, women were also recruited to free men for the Front. Since 1943, the Reich Labour Service was under the direct command of Hitler, the workmen laboured for the Wehrmacht. After the war, the building was used by the Allies; today the building is empty.

4
„Track 17" Memorial
⌂ Hirsch, Lorch & Wendel, 1991 → S-Bahnhof Grunewald, Map B3 Ⓢ Grunewald Grunewald station lies at the edge of the woods in a residential area of villas. Protests by residents against the long queues of Jewish prisoners waiting to be deported from here, were less likely. Today, access to the memorial to the deportations is via the very ramp that tens of thousands of Jewish Berliners had to cross. At the freight station they were put in cattle wagons and taken to the SS-concentra-

1 Eagle in front of the House of German Sports

tion camps in Eastern Europe. The Reich Railways billed the Reich Security Central Office 4 pfennigs per „passenger" with a group discount starting from 400 people upwards. The memorial is made of several cast steel plates embedded in the platform, representing the different transports. Engraved are the date, the number of people and the destination of the trains.

5
Leni Riefenstahl's House

⌂ Hans Ostler, 1936 → Heydenstraße 30, Map B3 Ⓢ Grunewald Leni Riefenstahl was born 22 August 1902 in Berlin. After a successful career as an actress she directed her first film in 1932, „**The Blue Light**". Commissioned by Hitler, she filmed the Nazi party rallies, producing propaganda films in documentary style, „**Victory of Faith**" (1933) and „**Triumph of the Will**" (1935). The highpoint of her career were the two films about the Olympics in Berlin, „**Festival of the Nations**" and „**Festival of Beauty**". The unusual camera angles and extreme close-ups, glorifying the human body, gained her worldwide recognition. It was at this time that her villa in Dahlem was built. The „Führer" and Joseph Goebbels were invited to the house-warming party. Tea was served in the Spanish atrium courtyard and plans were made: in Babelsberg near Potsdam, Albert Speer had earmarked an area of 20 000 square meters for the future „**Riefenstahl Studios**". Her collaboration with the Nazi regime led to frequent criticism after the war and she could continue her work only on a modest scale. On 9 September 2003 Leni Riefenstahl died at the age of 101 years. The Building today is private property.

6
Arno Breker's Studio

⌂ Hans Freese, 1942 → Käuzchensteig 10, Map B3 Ⓢ Podbielskiallee The studio was built especially for the „Führer's" favourite sculptor in 1942. Working in close collaboration with the Inspector General for Buildings, Albert Speer, Breker received many commissions for the Reich and, on Hitler's explicit wish, was involved in the „Germania" plans. Breker produced busts of many Nazi celebrities as well as the monumental sculptures for, among others, the ▷ New Reich Chancellery and the ▷ Reichssportfeld. But by 1943 the studio could no longer be used due to bomb damage, and Breker moved to the gigantic „**Arno Breker Sculpture Workshops Ltd**" in Wriezen, northeast of Berlin. After the war, Breker again was well in demand in Germany and abroad. The Berlin studio is now the home of the Bernhard-Heiliger Foundation, and the Brücke Museum is close by.

7
Museum of the Allied Powers

→ Clayallee 135, Map B3 Ⓤ Oskar-Helene-Heim ⌚ Tue – Sun 10 – 18 The former US Army cinema and library was converted into a museum when the US troops left Berlin in 1992. Exhibits showing the history of the Western Allies after 1945 include one of the planes used during the Berlin Airlift and an original guard cabin from Checkpoint Charlie. A few hundred meters south, on Clay Allee 170, is the extensive complex of the former „Regional Air Command III of the Reich Capital Berlin". Since 1945 the building was used as headquarters by the US forces under General Lucius D. Clay, who here organized the airlift during the Soviet blockade of Berlin in 1948. The US Consulate General is housed here, until the completion of the new US Embassy at Pariser Platz.

8
SS „Comradeship" Housing Development

⌂ Hans Gerlach, 1939 → Selmaplatz, Map B3 Ⓤ Krumme Lanke In 1937, the SS started to build 600 houses in the idyllic countryside of nearby Grunewald for members of the „racial elite". Architect Hans Gerlach agreed his plans with the SS „Central Office for Race and Resettlement". The houses were to be „**simple and true, while displaying decency and dignity**". The detached, semi-detached and terraced houses,

6 Entrance to Breker's atelier

8 Houses in the SS housing development

7 French exhibition in the Allied Museum

1 Murellen-Gorge near the Amphitheater

4 „Track 17" Memorial

8 SS detached houses

10 Development site of the German nuclear bomb

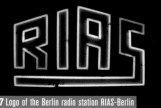
7 Logo of the Berlin radio station RIAS-Berlin

Himmler's Black Order

Heinrich Himmler 1900–1945

As Reichsführer (National Leader) of the SS, Heinrich Himmler was Hitler's most powerful henchman and directly responsible for the genocide of the European Jews. He often put in personal appearances, such as in Auschwitz, where he inspected the running of industrialized mass murder and showed great concern over the „working conditions" of his „Skull" camp guard units (Totenkopfverbände). As one of the promoters of the doctrine of „Aryan supremacy", Himmler tried to make his SS a Germanic master order according to the ideal of the Praetorian Guard of ancient Rome, the germ cell of the future race of heroes. Himmler was a fanatic and ruthless perpetrator of the „final solution to the Jewish question" and ordered the sterilization of men and women who did not conform to his ideal. Opponents of the regime were to be fought and exterminated. The sign of the swastika and the cult of the SS were for him the outer signs of a „Germanic holy order" which was to have its holy shrine at the Wewelsburg near Paderborn. At the end of the war Himmler tried to initiate negotiations for peace terms, and consequently Hitler dismissed him from all posts. Himmler fled, under a false name, and captured by the British. On 23 May 1945, Himmler avoided facing responsibility for his deeds by swallowing a poison capsule.

Dutch recruitment poster: „People of the Netherlands! For your Honor and Conscience – against Bolshevism. The Waffen-SS is calling you!" Right: Himmler with his daughter Gudrun.

The Waffen-SS (Armed Forces of the SS)

The SS (Schutzstaffel) was originally set up as Hitler's personal bodyguard unit and part of the SA. From 1934 the SS had a paramilitary unit, which emerged from the „Leibstandarte-SS Adolf Hitler" (the original bodyguard unit): the SS „Skull" units (Totenkopfverbände) and the combat troops (Verfügungstruppe). With the beginning of the Second World War, Himmler introduced the name Waffen-SS (armed SS). By 1945 the Waffen-SS numbered more than 900 000. The strict racial recruitment criteria of the beginnings had to be abandoned during the course of the war due to the high losses. Volunteers and forcibly recruited members of the „Germanic" divisions from Scandinavia, France, the Netherlands and Belgium, were followed by Ukrainians, Croats, Balts, even Moslems and Indians. SS soldiers would be recognized by their characteristic camouflage uniform and the blood group tattooed under the arm, a „**reference code of blood brotherhood and bloody reign**" (Erich Kästner). The fully motorized elite units were excellently equipped, often acting independently of the Wehrmacht and feared by the Allied troops because of their fanatical fighting spirit and sense of martyrdom. Their military successes are overshadowed by the countless atrocities they committed. The „Waffen-SS" fought during the assault of the Soviet Union with excessive brutality and are known to have shot civilians, but also fellow soldiers suspected of desertion or defeatism, right up to the very last day of the war. After the war, the Allied powers declared the SS a criminal organization.

still standing today, were allocated according to rank. All of them today are private property.

9
Kaiser Wilhelm Institute for Anthropology, Human Genetics and Eugenistics

⌂ Carl Sattler, 1927 → Ihnestraße 22–24, Map B3 Ⓤ Oskar-Helene-Heim
From 1927 to 1942, Eugen Fischer was Director of the Institute and played a major part in the formu-lation of the Nazi law on sterilization „for the prevention of progeny afflicted with hereditary diseases".

His successor was Ottmar von Verschuer, an authority on research on twins. Verschuers assistant, Josef Mengele, camp „doctor" in Auschwitz, supplied him with human specimens in large quantities. Favourite „research objects" were Jews, gypsies, people with deform-ities and, above all, twins, all specially selected by Mengele at the ramp at Auschwitz.

Blood samples, skeletons, aborted fetuses, children's heads, testicles and eye balls were sent to the Kaiser Wilhelm Institute. The specimens were used for research on what the Nazis understood by human genetics.

10
Kaiser Wilhelm Institute for Physics

⌂ 1936 → Boltzmannstraße 18–20, Map B3 Ⓤ Oskar-Helene-Heim
Like Max Planck and Otto Hahn, Werner Heisenberg was one of the few physicists who did not emigrate after the Nazis came to power.
Towards the end of 1938, Otto Hahn and Fritz Straßmann discovered that the splitting of a uranium atom sets free enormous quantities of energy. The possibility of a chain reaction, creating an explosive of unheard-of power, was of great interest to the military. After the beginning of the war, the Army Ordnance Office intensified the program for the „use of fission energy" and made Heisenberg leader of the „**Uranium Project**". In 1941 he became director of the Kaiser Wilhelm Institute in Dahlem.

Based on his theory of a **uranium machine** he managed to construct a precursor to a nuclear reactor, and on 4 June 1942, the „**Uranium Project**" was presented to the Minister of Armaments, Albert Speer. Heisenberg spoke about the possibility of developing an atomic bomb, but emphasized the enormous technical challenge and the immense costs.

„Since September 1941 we saw a clear road towards the atom bomb." (Werner Heisenberg)

At the beginning of 1945 the final large-scale trials were conducted in Southern Germany where Heisenberg nearly succeeded in building a functioning reactor. The Physicist Carl Friedrich von Weizsäcker, who participated in the project, stated on 8 August 1945: „**History will record that the Germans had a technically feasible uranium machine.**"

11
Headquarters of the „Leibstandarte-SS Adolf Hitler"/ Federal Archives

⌂ Fleischinger & Voigtel, 1878 → Finkkensteinallee 63, Map B4 Ⓢ Lichterfelde-West
The foundation stone for the former „Imperial Cadet School" was laid on 1 September 1873.
From 1881 the first electric tram, built by Siemens & Halske, linked the military complex with the railway station

Gothic Typeface

Is this the word „Gestapo" or the word „Gestaltung" (design)? The fractured typeface and the red and white colors

immediately suggest a connection to the „Third Reich". The Gothic typeface was used widely by the National Socialists up to 1940, when suddenly, on 3 January 1941, its use was forbidden by a decree issued by Bormann on Hitler's order, because in the annexed territories it had led to confusion.

The bizarre ban was justified officially on the grounds that the typeface was in fact a variation of the **„Schwabach Jewish script"**. The Latin Antiqua was to be the official typeface from now on. The gothic type hence disappeared from all newspapers, books and posters. The ban is no longer in force, but there is a marked reluctance to „rehabilitate" it.

Bormann's decree of 1941: the letterhead remains in Gothic type despite the ban!

Lichterfelde-Ost. When the Nazis came to power, the „Leibstandarte-SS Adolf Hitler", an elite SS-unit put up their headquarters here in 1933. In June 1934, during the murder of Röhm and other SA leaders, numerous people were shot here.

Under the command of SS-Officer Sepp Dietrich, the „Leibstandarte" became the official representational guard of the „Third Reich".

The unit grew to divisional strength by 1940 and was feared because of their brutal methods. After fighting in the Battle of the Bulge 1944/45, they were moved to Hungary and finally surrendered in Austria in 1945. After the war, the US military took over the buildings and called them „Andrews Barracks".

Since 1995 it has become the home of the Federal Archives of Germany. At the entrance gates, two stone SS-soldiers stood guard here. They are still there, covered up by concrete.

12
SS Economic and Administrative Central Office
→ Unter den Eichen 128–135, Map B3
Ⓢ Botanischer Garten

This was the central office for the management of the concentration and extermination camps as well as the central office of the SS business enterprises. Its director was Waffen-SS General Oswald Pohl, who took over in 1942.

Hundreds of thousands of concentration camp inmates were killed in the **„extermination through work"** program, working as slaves for the German armaments industry.

Pohl was responsible for transferring the plundered assets the murdered Jews, including hair, clothes, jewelry and foreign currencies, to his office's bank account.

In the eastern courtyard of the office building, prisoners from the ▷**Sachsenhausen concentration camp** were housed in a hut. Today the Building is empty, a memorial plaque recalls the history of this ordinary-looking building.

13
Bauhaus School Berlin
→ Birkbuschstraße, Ecke Siemens-
straße 27, Map B3 Ⓢ Lankwitz
In 1919 the Public Bauhaus School was
founded in Weimar, and was to become
a model for modern education in architecture, industrial design, photography
and art. The right wing regional government forced the founder Walter Gropius
to move the internationally renowned
school to Dessau in 1925, where the
Nazis (governing party in the region)
closed it down in 1932. Mies van der
Rohe found a new home for the school
in Berlin-Steglitz, in a former telephone
factory.
On 11 April 1933 the police and SA
staged a raid on the building. Under
the pretext of looking for communist
propaganda material, the building was
searched and sealed off. Later the
school was closed down for good.
At least 12 members of the Bauhaus
died in concentration camps.
Exhibitions are put on in the Bauhaus
Archive in Klingelhöferstraße 14, designed by Gropius in 1964.

14
Fritz Lang's House
⌂ Wassili Luckhardt, 1930 → Schorle-
merstraße 7a, Map C3 Ⓢ Lichterfelde-
Ost The director, world-famous for his
film **„Metropolis"**, lived here until his
emigration in 1933. While his works

were banned in Germany, **„The Nibe-
lungs"** remained one of Hitler's favourite
films. The Minister for Propaganda,
Joseph Goebbels, therefore tried to offer
the post of Reich Head of Film to Lang,
but could not prevent Lang from leaving
for Hollywood.
Lang's wife, Thea von Harbou, who had
written the scripts for Lang's films,
remained in Germany, sued for divorce
in the same year and later joined the
Nazi party.

15
Heinz Rühmann's House
⌂ 1936 → Am Kleinen Wannsee 15,
Map A4 Ⓢ Wannsee Since the 1930s,
Heinz Rühmann was one of the most
popular and best-paid actors of the
German Reich. With the beginning of
the war, the amateur pilot was drafted
to the Luftwaffe, if mainly for propaganda reasons.
He was more or less exempted from
service and was able to continue
making films for public entertainment,
such as **„Quax, the Crash-Pilot"**. Due to
„lack of respect for the authorities" his
comedy film **„Feuerzangenbowle"** was
banned in 1944.
A visit to Hitler, however, led to its
release. Rühmann remained in Berlin
for the final days of the war. After
the war he was able to continue his
career. He died on 3 October 1994
at the age of 92.

11 Entrance to the swimming stadium of the „Leibstandarte-SS Adolf Hitler"

GERMANY: MAP OF THE OCCUPATION
KARTE DER BESATZUNGS

Gestaltung und Vertrieb mit Genehmigung der Militär-Regierung - Atlanta-Service Frankfurt am Main - Generalvertretung und Auslieferung für Bayern: Johannes Sünnecke, Frankfurt am Main.

16
„Wannsee Conference" Memorial

⌂ Paul Baumgarten, 1914 → Am Großen Wannsee 56–58, Map A4
Ⓢ Wannsee ⏲ Mon–Sun 10–18

On 31 July 1941 the head of the Security Service Reinhard Heydrich was asked by Hermann Göring to initiate plans for a „comprehensive solution to the European Jewish question". On 20 January 1942 Heydrich chaired a conference in the villa on Wannsee, where representatives from Reich authorities, NSDAP and SS planned the „final solution", the extermination of at least 11 million European Jews. Until 1945, Berlin-Wannsee was one of the most important sites for the SS-Reich Security Service. Walter Schellenberg, SS-head of international security, and Otto Ohlendorf, SS-head of internal security, had their offices here. In 1992 the villa has become a memorial and documentation center to the „Wannsee Conference" and the Holocaust.

17
Schwanenwerder Island

→ Inselstraße, Grunewald, Map B3
Ⓢ Nikolassee Schwanenwerder Island was a popular place with the NDSAP leaders, who bought up, in most cases, unlawfully confiscated villas at prime sites. At Inselstraße 20–22 the building of a villa for **Adolf Hitler** was planned. His personal physician, **Theodor Morell**, lived next door at No. 16. **Albert Speer** bought a site on Inselstraße 7 where he planned to build a spacious villa. He and his family resided in a rented villa on Inselstraße 18; he also owned another house at Schopenhauerstraße 21 on nearby Schlachtensee.

LEGEND · ERKLÄRUNG

BOUNDARIES · GRENZEN:

GERMANY
DEUTSCHLAND **1937**

OCCUPATION AREAS
BESATZUNGSZONEN **1945**

PROVINCES · PROVINZEN

ZONES · ZONEN:

AMERICAN ZONE · AMERIKANISCHE ZONE
BRITISH ZONE · BRITISCHE ZONE
FRENCH ZONE · FRANZÖSISCHE ZONE
RUSSIAN ZONE · RUSSISCHE ZONE
POLISH TERRITORY · POLNISCHES GEBIET

Alle Rechte vorbehalten.

Einzelpreis: RM 0.30

Escape and Expulsion

The Second World War led to an unparalleled movement of refugees across Europe. As decided by the Allies in Yalta and the Potsdam Conference in ▷ **Cecilienhof Castle**, the territory of Poland was moved westward by 250 km. In this process, Poland gained 114 000 square kilometers – to make up for the 180 000 square kilometers that Poland was to cede to the Soviet Union. In the following years, about 14 million Germans were forcefully expelled from Eastern Europe and had to pay the price for Hitler's crimes.

The British Nobel prize winner Bertrand Russell stated in a letter to the London „Times": „**In Eastern Europe now mass deportations are being carried out by our allies on an unprecedented scale, and an apparently deliberate attempt is being made to exterminate many millions of Germans (...)."**

18 Cecilienhof Castle

Minister of Propaganda **Joseph Goebbels** lived with his wife Magda and their six children at Inselstraße 8–14 (today: Aspen Institute). The former outhouse, where servants and SS guards lived, is now used by the river police. The shelter Goebbels had built as protection against air raids still exists. In autumn 1943 however he left his Wannsee villa and moved to his palatial ▷ **country seat** at **Lanke on Bogensee** (north of Berlin).

18
Cecilienhof Castle / Hotel

⌂ Paul Schulze-Naumburg, 1917
→ Im Neuen Garten, Potsdam, Map A4
Ⓢ Potsdam Hauptbahnhof ⏰ Tue – Sun 9 – 17 On 2 August 1945, the heads of government of the victorious powers, Harry Truman, Winston Churchill and Josef Stalin met at Cecilienhof Castle to decide on the future fate of Germany.

Erich Kästner noted in his diary on 19 May 1945: „**First at the Elbe, then at the gates of Berlin, the Western Allies wait by the open doors and say to Stalin: 'Please, after you'. What's the point of this ill-conceived courtesy? Do they think that democracy is such a good thing it needs no recommendation? Do they think that competition is unnecessary for the defeated? Or not the done thing? This would be a mistake with enormous and irrevocable consequences. The democratic world has to be careful not to squander its victory. The first weeks after a capitulation are precious minutes of history. They can neither be postponed nor taken up again at a later date."**
On the other hand, since 1944 plans for an rearmament of Germany had been discussed by the western allies, in regard of future frictions with the Soviet Union. The castle today is a luxury

22 Airforce Museum of the Federal Armed Forces of Germany

13 Memorial plaque at the former Bauhaus Berlin

17 House of the SS guards on Schwanenwerder

21 House „Italy" of the „Hitler Youth"

16 „Wannsee Conference" location

29 Arms and munitions factory

19 Grave of Frederick the Great

hotel, the conference room and offices of the so-called „Potsdam Conference", where the demilitarization of Germany and its division into occupational zones were decided, are open to the public.

19
Grave of Frederick the Great of Prussia
→ Schloss Sanssouci Ⓢ Potsdam Hauptbahnhof, Map A 4

In March 1943, on Hitler's orders, the coffins of Frederick the Great and his father Friedrich Wilhelm I were evacuated from Potsdam. They were first taken to a bunker at the Airforce headquarters in Wildpark Werder (north of Potsdam). With the advance to the Red Army it was decided to store them in a potassium mine near Nordhausen (Thuringia).

In spite of the secrecy, US troops discovered the coffins after the war. After a temporary interment at Burg Hohenzollern (southwestern part of Germany), Frederick the Great was finally buried, according to his original wishes, in a simple grave covered by a stone slab at Schloss Sanssouci on 17 August 1991.

In memory of the fact that he introduced the potato to Prussia, there is always one lying on his grave.

20
Albert Einstein's House
⌂ Konrad Wachsmann, 1929 → Waldstraße 7, Caputh, Map A 4 🕐 Sat-Sun 13-16 Here, close to Schwielow-See in Caputh, Albert Einstein had a small summer cottage built, while his home in the city was in Haberlandstraße 5. Here he sailed and received friends from all over the world. He also went to Potsdam to the Einstein Tower, a research institute with a solar observatory built for him in 1924 by renowned architect Erich Mendelsohn.

When Hitler came to power, Einstein's houses were searched in spring 1933. Einstein, who was in the USA at that time, renounced his German citizenship in writing on 28 March 1933; he never returned to Berlin. His books were ceremoniously burnt on Opernplatz (Bebelplatz), his possessions and assets confiscated.

The summer house, now under preservation order, can be visited at weekends. The Einstein Tower, well worth a visit, is now part of the „Science Park Albert Einstein" on Telegrafenberg.

21
House „Italy" of the „Hitler Youth"
⌂ Fritz Winter, 1937 → Breitenhornweg 54, Gatow, Map B 3 The house of the „Hitler Youth" (Hitlerjugend – HJ), named after the German „Axis" partner, was built as part of the „Youth Building Program". It was used as a guesthouse and its style reflects the Nazi idea of representational architecture.

The „Hitler Youth" was the Nazi party organization for the German youth and was part of Hitler's concept of ideological control over all areas of German life. Since 1933, a general compulsory youth service was introduced under Baldur von Schirach, similar to the labour and military service. National Socialist education and pre-military training were the main aims. Towards the end of the war, countless „Hitler youth"- boys were used to operate Anti Aircraft Guns or were sent to the combat zones as **„the Führers last levy"**.

22
Gatow Airforce Academy/ Airforce Museum of the German Federal Armed Forces
⌂ 1935 → Kladower Damm 182-188, Gatow, Map A 3 🕐 Tue-Sun 9-17 Gatow airfield linked the last remaining air corridor into the center of Berlin up to the last days of the „Third Reich"; it was taken by the Soviet troops on 27 April 1945. After the war, the airfield was used by the British Royal Air Force, and from 1994 by the Bundeswehr. Hangar 3 houses an exhibition on the history of the German air force. Among the items displayed is a **Fokker Triplane**, belonging to the **„Red Baron"**, Manfred von Richthofen.

23
Berlin-Spandau Allied War Criminal Prison

⌂ 1878 → Wilhelmstraße 23, Berlin-Spandau, Map A3 Ⓢ Spandau The extensive complex was erected as a military prison in 1878 and requisitioned by the Allied forces in 1946. On 18 July 1947 the seven men sentenced to detention in the Nürnberg war trials arrived:

Rudolf Hess, Walther Funk and Erich Raeder (life imprisonment), Baldur von Schirach and Albert Speer (20 years imprisonment), Constantin von Neurath (15 years), Karl Dönitz (10 years).

After some amnesties and Speer's release in 1966, Rudolf Hess remained the last prisoner in Spandau. On 17 August 1987 he committed suicide, and shortly after the prison was pulled down. Today there is a shopping center on the site.

24
Döberitz Military Training Grounds

⌂ 1713 → Hamburger Chaussee, Dallgow-Döberitz, Map A3 Here, on Germany's oldest military training grounds, Friedrich Wilhelm I conducted field exercises in 1713. Also Frederick the Great of Prussia used this area to train his numerous soldiers (his army had in the meantime grown to one of Europe's greatest military units).

Just before World War I this was the birthplace of the German Airforce. During the Olympic Games 1936, the military riding competitions took place here. Shortly after, the pilots of the Condor Legion from the nearby air force barracks were sent to Spain. The fighter group No 1 „Freiherr von Richthofen" was stationed here at the beginning of the war to protect Berlin. Used by the Soviets after the war, the barracks are nowadays used by the Federal Armed Forces of Germany, while the rest of the area is being developed for walkers and cyclists.

25
Olympic Village

⌂ Werner March, 1936 → Hamburger Chaussee, Dallgow-Döberitz, Map A3 ⏲ Every first Sat of the month 10–14 According to the organizational committee, the Olympic village of the summer games 1936 was to convey an impression of the appealing mentality of the German people through architecture and landscaping.

The international athletes reacted positively to their surroundings and praised the perfect organization and catering arrangements.

The Nazi Cultural Committee put on events in the „Hindenburg-House", and in an attempt to familiarize the guests with German geography, the 145 living quarters were named after German cities and arranged according to the map of Germany.

Following the games, the site was used as army barracks, first by the Wehrmacht, after 1945 by the Soviet troops deployed in Germany. While structurally sound, the houses and sports halls, now under preservation order, are empty since 1994 and in danger of becoming dilapidated. The association Historia Elstal conducts guided walking tours (after pre-registration).

26
Workers' Village
Great Hall

⌂ Albert Speer, 1938 → Stadtrandstraße, Spandau, Map A3 Ⓢ Spandau The workers' village was planned by the Inspector General for Building Albert Speer as a model housing project for the 8 000 German workers who were to build the ▷ **Great Hall**.

Of the 25 planned buildings, only nine got finished due to lack of building materials. In 1942, when construction work on the ▷ **Great Hall** was suspended, forced labourers were housed here.

The surviving buildings have been integrated into the premises of the hospital Waldkrankenhaus in Spandau.

23 Remains of the prison for war criminals

25 Olympic swimming hall

25 Hurdle on Jesse Owens' track

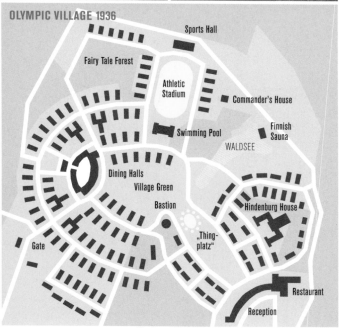

OLYMPIC VILLAGE 1936

Sports Hall

Fairy Tale Forest

Athletic Stadium

Commander's House

Swimming Pool

Finnish Sauna

WALDSEE

Dining Halls

Village Green

Bastion

Hindenburg House

Gate

„Thing-platz"

Restaurant

Reception

(Hamburger Chaussee)

25 Derelict house in the Olympic Village of 1936

The „Miracle Weapon"

In 1937, after the „Army Research Institute" moved from Kummersdorf to Peenemünde, up to 20 000 people were working on the development of a carrier missile. **In 1942 a German A4-rocket managed for the first time to leave the earth atmosphere, reaching a height of 90 km.** As the first long-range rocket in the world it reached quadruple sonic speed, and was then mass-produced as the V2 (Vergeltungswaffe 2 – Reprisal Weapon 2). In the tunnels of the satellite concentration camp „Dora-Mittelbau" in south-east Germany, thousands of forced labourers worked in rocket production. In the course of the war a total of 12 000 V2s were launched towards Britain, Belgium and the Netherlands.

While relatively unimportant in military terms, the psychological impact of the „miracle weapon", hitting its target without warning, was immense. Towards late 1944 von Braun constructed the models A9/A10, which in the later development stages would have been manned. They were to reach as far as the USA. The later moon rockets were based on this design. Today, the armaments factory Peenemünde is also seen as the cradle of space flight, where German scientists started the space age.

Wernher von Braun 1912–1977

While studying engineering at the Berlin University of Technology, von Braun became a member of the „Society for Space Travel" of Hermann Oberth. At the age of 27, von Braun joined the SS and was made Technical Director of the missile weapons project at the „Army Research Institute" (Heeresversuchsanstalt) in Peenemünde, where he worked till March 1945.

Together with 500 employees he surrendered to the American troops who shipped the remaining missiles and plans to the USA. The German engineers now worked for the USA and in 1960 von Braun became director of the NASA George C. Marshall Space Flight Center. There he led the development of the large space launch vehicles, Saturn I, IB, and V, and is known as the father of the moon rocket. At the beginning of the 1970s, he was made vice-director of NASA. After his death in 1977 he was honoured with a statue and the von Braun Arena in Huntsville, Alabama.

Launch of a V2-Rocket in the Netherlands near The Hague, targeted on London

27
Airforce Infantry Regiment „General Göring"/Julius Leber Barracks

⌂ Oberbaurat Schneidt, 1939 → Kurt-Schumacher-Damm 41, Map B3
Ⓤ Kurt-Schumacher-Platz The former barracks of the Airforce Infantry Regiment „General Göring", built at a cost of 81 million Reichsmark, was one of the most prestigious military building projects in Berlin during the „Third Reich". After the war, the French Army used the site as headquarters. Today, it has been renamed as Julius Leber Barracks, housing the Special Air Mission Wing of the Federal Armed Forces of Germany. Julius Leber was one of the conspirators of the German resistance against Hitler and was designated as Chancel-lor or Minister of the Interior after the successful coup. He was sentenced by the ▷„People's Court" and executed on 20 October 1944.

28
Anti-War Museum

→ Brüsselerstraße 21, Map C3
Ⓤ Seestraße ⏲ Mon–Sun 16–20
In 1925, the pacifist Ernst Friedrich founded the first anti-war museum in Berlin (on Fisher Isle). The SA destroyed the museum in 1933 and established a notorious torture center there. The museum presents at its actual location a permanent exhibition of documents, photos and equipment demonstrating the horrors of war.

29
German Munitions and Arms Factory

⌂ Gontard, 1906 → Eichborndamm 103–187, Map B2 Ⓢ Eichborndamm The impressive red-brick facade was enlarged by Alfred Kühne in 1918, in keeping with the original building. During the Second World War, a workforce of conscripted labourers produced arms and munitions for the Wehrmacht; a plaque commemorates this fact today. The German Office for Information about Former Soldiers of the Wehrmacht and parts of the Berlin state archives are established here.

30
Soviet War Memorial Schönholzer Heide

⌂ K. A. Sobolyev, 1949 → Volkspark Schönholzer Heide, Map C2 Ⓢ Wilhelmsruh At this gigantic site are buried 13 200 Soviet soldiers, killed during the Battle of Berlin. In the center of the memorial stands a larger-than-life bronze statue of a Russian mother, lamenting her dead son.

31
Rocket Research Station of the Army Ordnance Office

⌂ 1932 → Kummersdorf, Map C4 Here at the test site in Kummersdorf, the first test range for liquid-fueled rockets was developed after the First World War. From 1923 onwards, the Army Ordnance Office conducted large-scale experiments with rockets. Gauging hoppers and launch pads were built, some of which can still be seen, serving as a model for the installation at Peenemünde. In 1933, Wernher von Braun and his crew completed the rocket „Aggregate 1" (A1), but it exploded before

---

„Nothing looks easier afterwards than the realization of a utopian idea." <small>(Wernher von Braun)</small>

---

the launch. One year later A2 lifted off and reached a height of 2 200 meters. A3, completed in 1936, was so large its launch would have endangered the surrounding buildings, and the site was moved to Peenemünde in 1937. Research on nuclear fission was also conducted at Kummersdorf. Remains of the test shelter, where the German atomic bomb (tested probably in March 1945 in Thuringia) was to be developed, have also survived. The Bürgerverein Kummersdorf-Gut offers guided walks (please register beforehand).

32
„Zeppelin": Supreme Command of the Army, Shelter Settlement „Maybach I and II"

⌂ 1938 → Zossen/Wünsdorf, Gutenbergstraße 9. Map C4
⏱ Mon–Fri 14–16, Sat–Sun 12–16, Garrison Museum: Mon–Fri 13–17, Sat–Sun 11–17 On this 6000 hectare military training ground, barracks were built for the Prussian army in 1900. Between 1937 and 1941 extensive shelter installations were erected for the Supreme Command of the German Army.

Under the code-name **„Zeppelin"** after the first letter of the nearby town of Zossen, the first communications shelter was put into operation. The general staff moved into the shelter settlement **„Maybach I"** and later **„Maybach II"**, named after the car manufacturer that also made tank engines.

The 24 shelter houses had four levels, two underground and two above ground. Covered by bricks and wooden cladding, they looked exactly like normal staff headquarters buildings, but in fact were made from high-grade reinforced concrete and had a bomb-proofed cellar ceiling.

The **„Zeppelin"** communications shelter, extending over three underground levels, was so massively built that it withstood all attacks intact. The walls are 1.6 meters thick, while the ceiling is made of 3 meters thick reinforced concrete. On top of that are 12 meters of soil, covered by another layer of 1 meter reinforced concrete. In this bunker the plans for the invasions of Belgium, the Netherlands, France, Greece, Yugoslavia, Denmark, Norway, Lybia and the Soviet Union were drawn up. Orders were sent out via a tele-communications network to the German armies in the whole of Europe.

After the war, the staff of Soviet Marshal Zhukov used the 590 hectare barracks complex. 40000 soldiers of the Red Army were stationed here, making it the most important garrison of the Soviet Armed Forces in Germany. For nearly a 100 years the site was a restricted area, but today the bunkers are open to visitors. The museum provides a view of the „Winkel" bunker and the history of this military site.

Bottom: One of the 19 „Winkel" air-raid shelter towers in Wünsdorf built according to plans by architect Leo Winkel. Hundreds of them were built all over Germany, and hardly any were destroyed due to their patented bomb-proof construction.

33
German-Russian Museum Karlshorst

⌂ 1938 → Zwieseler Straße 4, Map C3 Ⓢ Karlshorst ⏱ Tue–Sun 10–18 The Wehrmacht signed the unconditional surrender at the headquarters of the Western forces in Reims on 7 May 1945, the ceremony was repeated on 8 May for the Soviet side in Berlin-Karlshorst by General Field Marshal Keitel on behalf of the German Reich.

These historic rooms are now the home of an exhibition on World War II with numerous original exhibits and some armored vehicles. There are also special exhibitions on German-Russian history.

32 Massive reinforced concrete gabled roof of a blasted bunker house in the „Maybach I" housing estate

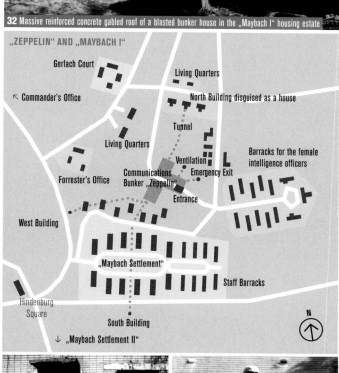

„ZEPPELIN" AND „MAYBACH I"

Gerlach Court

↖ Commander's Office

Living Quarters

North Building disguised as a house

Tunnel

Living Quarters

Barracks for the female
intelligence officers

Ventilation

Forrester's Office

Communications
Bunker „Zeppelin"

Emergency Exit

Entrance

West Building

„Maybach Settlement"

Hindenburg
Square

Staff Barracks

South Building

↓ „Maybach Settlement II"

N

32 Zossen was once an Olympic training post of the USSR

32 Statue of Lenin in Wünsdorf

32 „Let the traditions of competition grow!"

35 Spin tower

35 View from spin tower

35 Large wind tunnel

39 Joseph Goebbels' country estate

45 Airforce test site, Rechlin

40 Göring's country estate „Carinhall", 1937

34
Forced Labour Camp Niederschöneweide

⌂ 1943 → Britzer, Köllnische, Rudower Straße, Map D3 Ⓢ Schöneweide
During World War II, there were more than 700 forced labor camps and about 30 satellite camps of the two ▷ **concentration camps Sachsenhausen** and **Ravensbrück** in the Berlin area. In 1993, among the blocks of flats, a former camp for 2 000 forced labourers was discovered, its barracks mostly still intact. Despite a preservation order, this „forgotten camp" is becoming derelict.

35
German Research Institute for Aviation

⌂ Brenner & Deutschmann, 1936 → Rudower Chaussee 4–6, Map C3 Ⓢ Adlershof On Count Zeppelin's recommendation the „German Research Center for Aviation" was established in 1912. The Berlin-Johannisthal airfield, the oldest in Germany, was chosen as a suitable site, and various research institutes and test sites were built. The Nazi regime intensified military research from 1933 onwards, and supported the Research Institute for Aviation with considerable sums from the ▷ **Reich Aviation Ministry,** particularly after the 4-year plan was announced in 1936. Arranged in the original sequence of tests, the spin tower or the wind tunnel show in exemplary fashion the cradle of German aviation research.

36
Memorial to the Köpenick Week of Blood in June 1933

→ Puchanstraße 12, Map D3 Ⓢ Köpenick ⏲ Tue, Wed 10–16, Thu 10–18, Sat 14–18 When the Nazis came to power, SA terror in Köpenick reached new heights during the days of 21 to 26 June 1933. Hundreds of political opponents were rounded up in the streets and taken to the Köpenick prison, SA headquarters or SA institutions, interrogated and brutally tortured. At least 24 citizens were murdered. Many of the severely injured victims died later, others disappeared without a trace. The prison building of 1901 documents the events during the Köpenick Week of Blood.

37
Seelow Heights Memorial

⌂ 1996 → Küstriner Straße 28a, Seelow, Map D3 ⏲ Tue–Sat 9–16.30
The Seelow Heights on the banks of the river Oder were considered the final easternward natural barrier protecting Berlin in the spring of 1945. 200 000 German soldiers and a division of collaborators were facing 900 000 advancing Red Army troops. The ▷ **Battle of Berlin** began, and after bitter fighting, the Soviet troops succeeded in breaking through on 17 April. About 70 000 Red Army soldiers and 12 000 German soldiers were killed here. The permanent exhibition of the memorial, overlooking the battlefield, contains photos, maps, equipment and some Russian tanks plus multiple rocket launchers (nicknamed „Stalin's organ pipes" in German).

38
„Seewerk" of the IG Farben AG

⌂ 1938 → Militärsiedlung 1, Falkenhagen, Map D3 ⏲ Sat 14.00 In 1938, the Army Ordnance Office commissioned the so-called „Seewerk" for the development of incendiary material in a wood 40 km east of Berlin. Since 1944 the installations were handed over to „IG-Farben" chemical industry giant on Hitler's personal command to develop a new weapon: the poison gas Sarin. With a monthly output of 500 tons, it would have been possible to depopulate cities like London completely. The poison gas was a purely German development and unknown to the Allies until the end of the war. The laboratories were already fully equipped, and production was due to start in the summer of 1945. Remains of the gigantic building project are the shells of power station, the production sites, the filling station plus rail connections and an extensive underground bunker system. The site, which was also used by the Soviets, can be viewed today.

The Concentration Camps

The idea of confining a particular group of people in camps was originally developed by the British, who set up camps in South Africa during the fight against the Boers in 1900. The first German concentration camps

tered inmates was 714 000, supervised by about 40 000 SS members. Of the 7 million prisoners in total only about 500 000 survived the terror and murder in the camps.

were established 1933 in Oranienburg and in Dachau. Soon after, the Nazis set up a dense network of concentration and extermination camps across the German Reich and later particularly in Poland.

Prisoners were used as cheap work slaves and became an economic factor of increasing importance for the armament industries. Camps such as Auschwitz, Sobibor and Treblinka are synonyms for state-sponsored genocide in an industrial format. Attempts to escape usually ended at the barbed wire fence. In January 1945 the figure of registered inmates was 714 000, supervised

Zyklon B

Zyklon B, hydrogen cyanide, was originally an insecticide. The highly poisonous gas was delivered since 1941 to Auschwitz and other camps in the form of small crystals which, when exposed to air, turned into a toxic gas. The crystals were inserted through a small opening into the „gas chambers". Zyklon B was produced by the Deutsche Gesellschaft für Schädlingsbekämpfung – DEGESCH (German Association for Pesticides), a subsidiary of the IG Farben Industries.

Top: Label of a Zyklon B can

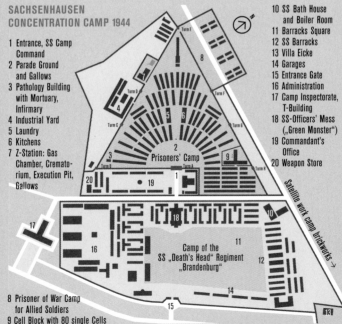

SACHSENHAUSEN CONCENTRATION CAMP 1944

1 Entrance, SS Camp Command
2 Parade Ground and Gallows
3 Pathology Building with Mortuary, Infirmary
4 Industrial Yard
5 Laundry
6 Kitchens
7 Z-Station: Gas Chamber, Crematorium, Execution Pit, Gallows

10 SS Bath House and Boiler Room
11 Barracks Square
12 SS Barracks
13 Villa Eicke
14 Garages
15 Entrance Gate
16 Administration
17 Camp Inspectorate, T-Building
18 SS-Officers' Mess („Green Monster")
19 Commandant's Office
20 Weapon Store

8 Prisoner of War Camp for Allied Soldiers
9 Cell Block with 80 single Cells

39
Joseph Goebbels' Country House

⌂ Schweitzer, Bartels, 1939 → Lanke
am Bogensee, Map D1 In 1936 Reich
Minister for Propaganda Joseph
Goebbels was given a large estate with
a block hut next to idyllic Bogensee
(vault lake) for his lifelong use. In 1939
he had a large, palatial country house
built on the site, which has survived
more or less in its original state. During
the summer months, Goebbels used to
live here with his family. In 1946 the
FDJ (Freie Deutsche Jugend/Free German Youth), the youth organization of
the Socialist State Party of the Soviet
Occupational Zone, SED (Sozialistische
Einheitspartei Deutschlands), took over
the complex and turned it into an isolated youth academy. Next door a monumental castle-like political training
school for the functionaries of the youth
organizations of the SED was established after 1951. For more than half
a century the people living in the area
were denied access to this location;
since 1999 the buildings are vacant and
the state of Berlin is looking for a buyer.

40
„Carinhall"

⌂ Ernst Sagebiel, 1934; Hetzel, Tuch
1937 → Großdöllner See, Wuckersee,
Schorfheide, Map D1 In 1936, Hitlers
second man Hermann Göring, most
powerful man in the Third Reich" next
to Hitler, and also Reich Hunting Master
ordered a monumental hunting lodge
to be built, which he called „Waldhof
Carinhall" in honor of his deceased wife,
swedish baroness Carin. Here he amass-
ed after 1938 the art treasures he had
plundered from all over Europe and
received guests of the state. As the
Red Army came closer and closer,

on 20 April 1945 about 420 lorries
left for Bavaria, stuffed with Göring's
precious loot. The lodge was blown up,
and without a glance back, Göring
commented: „This is the kind of thing
one has to do as a crown prince," and
went on to join Hitler's last birthday
party in the ▷ New Reich Chancellery.
A few shelters, cellars and the guard
house at the gate have survived and
also the guest house, which at present
accomodates a hotel.

41
Sachsenhausen
Concentration Camp

⌂ 1936 → Straße der Nationen 22,
Oranienburg, Map B1 ⊕ Tue–Sun
8.30–18.00 This „model" concentration
camp, designed by SS architects, was
erected by prisoners from the Emsland
camps in 1936. Up until the end of the
war, 200 000 inmates from 40 countries
were imprisoned here. Tens of thousands
were murdered or died of hunger and
disease. At the end of the war, most
of the inmates were forced in so-called
„death marches" to move northwest
(to the Baltic), while the remaining
3 000 were liberated by the Soviet army
on 22 April 1945.

41 North wall at the Sachsenhausen concentration camp

41 Entrance to Sachsenhausen concentration camp, tower A

41 Crematorium at Sachsenhausen concentration camp

41 Entrance gate to Sachsenhausen concentration camp

41 SS officers' mess („Green Monster")

41 Instruments of torture at Sachsenhausen concentration camp

41 Death zone at the concentration camp wall

41 Ramp in the morgue of the concentration camp

In the „T-Building" was the central office for all concentration camps in the German territories, the **„Inspektion der Konzentrationslager"** (IKL). SS officials at their desks decided on the nutrition, housing, punishment and killing of hundreds of thousands of human beings. Today, there is an exhibition in the former office of the head of the ILK, Theodor Eicke. From 1945 to 1950, the Soviet secret service NKVD used the camp, renamed as **„Special Camp 7"**. Of the 60 000 Wehrmacht soldiers, Nazis, anti-communists and SED-opponents interned here, at least 13 000 died.

The memorial set up in 1961 by the GDR government made no mention of a special Soviet camp. According to a design by Daniel Libeskind, the neighboring site of the former army camp of the SS „Death's Head"-Regiment „Brandenburg" is to be incorporated into the memorial. Many of the surviving buildings, like the SS officers mess (called the **„green monster"** by the inmates), are becoming derelict.

42
Satellite Work Camp Brickworks

⌂ 1941 → Bernauer Straße, Oranienburg, Map B1 In 1938 the SS – in collaboration with and on request by Albert Speer, Inspector General of Construction in the Reich Capital Berlin – had prisoners from the ▷ **Sachsenhausen concentration camp** set up what were to be the world's largest brickworks and, from 1940, a workshop for natural stone cladding.

In the satellite work camp, building material for Hitler's and Speer's monumental building project „Germania" was produced under murderous working conditions. The camp was destroyed by air raids in 1945. A history park is planned for the site.

43
Oranienburg
Concentration Camp

⌂ 1933 → Berliner Straße 20–21, Oranienburg, Map B1 In march 1933, immediately after Hitler came to power,

the SA opened up one of the first concentration camps in Germany in a disused brewery in the center of Oranienburg. Mainly social democrats and communists from the capital were detained here, 3 000 people in total. Beatings, sadistic torture and other cruelties were daily routine. By the time the camp was closed in July 1934, at least 16 prisoners had been killed. In 1944 the camp was destroyed in a bombing raid. Today, a plaque marks the site of these terrible events.

44
Ravensbrück Concentration Camp

⌂ 1939 → Straße der Nationen, Fürstenberg, Map B1 ⊙ Tue–Sun, 9–17 On the banks of Lake Schwedtsee, in view of the spa town of Fürstenberg, the largest concentration camp for women was erected in 1939. Here, the SS imprisoned more than 132 000 women and children, but also 20 000 men.

Tens of thousands of prisoners from more than forty nations were murdered or died of hunger, disease or through medical experiments. The camp included an industrial complex for the SS-owned Company for Textile and Leather Production (Texled), a Siemens complex with 20 production sites as well as the youth concentration camp Uckermark for female delinquents. Since late 1944 a gas chamber existed, where up to 6 000 people were murdered. Here in Ravensbrück, female prisoners were selected for work in the SS and prison brothels in other concentration camps. Instead of being released, as promised, after their six months of forced prostitution, the women were returned to Ravensbrück.

At the end of the war, tens of thousands of prisoners were forced to walk to the northwest in the so-called „death marches". On 30 April 1945 the Red Army liberated about 3 000 sick prisoners who had been left behind. Today, the Ravensbrück Memorial provides information on the history of the

The Swastika

The swastika (a Sanskrit symbol meaning „something good") was a sign of good luck in prehistory, symbolizing a turning sun wheel. It was found mainly in Europe and Asia. In Germanic folk art it symbolizes Thor's hammer. In Buddhism it brings bad luck if not held horizontally. At the beginning of the 19th century, it was used by the Gymnastics Movement to express its ties with the ordinary citizens of a Germany divided into countless states and ruled by the aristocracy.

By the 1920s, the members of the extreme-right-wing Freikorps (paramilitary units) carried the symbol on their steel helmets, giving it a nationalistic and anti-Semitic meaning. Adolf Hitler probably came across the swastika for the first time in the racist Ostara magazines edited in Vienna by Joseph Lanz von Liebenfels.
He adapted it for the Nazi party and personally designed the Nazi swastika flag. After his rise to power, this was declared the sole national flag.

> „Red stands for the socialist ideal of our movement, white for the nationalist ideal, while the swastika symbolizes our mission to fight for the victory of the Aryan people." (Adolf Hitler)

The swastika, together with the Reich eagle, became the national emblem instead of the black-red-gold tricolor of the Weimar Republic, which the Nazi hated as a symbol of democracy. After the war, the Allies and later the FRG and the GDR banned the swastika. Today the use of this anti-Semitic and neo-fascist symbol is a punishable offence.

camp, and the buildings have been converted into an education and meeting center for young people.

46
„White Houses"
Airforce Test Site
⌂ 1934 → Am Claassee 1, Rechlin, Map B1 ⏱ Mon–Sun 10–16
Since the beginning of the allied air-raids on Germany in 1940, the Nazi leadership tried to improve protection for the German population against bombing raids. At a secret test site near Rechlin, bunker towers were built, disguised by brick cladding and nicknamed **„white houses"** by local residents. They were probably developed as bomb-proofed model houses for the future world capital „Germania". The Museum of Aviation Technology in Rechlin provides more information on the history of the former test site.

47
Museum of the Death March in the Below Woods
⌂ 1981 → Belower Damm 1, Wittstock, Map A1 ⏱ Tue–Sun 9–16
The evacuation of the ▷ **concentration camps Sachsenhausen** and **Ravensbrück** began on 21 April 1945. About 33 000 of the remaining 38 000 prisoners were forced to start marching north-west. Many prisoners died from the cold, physical exhaustion or were murdered by the SS. They marched along different routes all eventually reaching Wittstock. From the 23 April 1945, around 16 000 prisoners were held in a camp near to Belower Wald, this is now the museum of the death marches. For nearly a week they camped in holes in the ground or home-made shelters without any food supply. During this time, they lived on nothing but bark and roots. About 800 people died in the first few days.
Till today, the marks and words carved into the trees testify to the prisoners' suffering. In its permanent exhibition, the Museum provides information on the death marches and displays objects left behind by the prisoners.

47
„Swastika Forest"

⌂ Förster Schmidt, 1938 → Kutzerower Wald, Zernikow, Map B1 It must have been a Nazi-faithful forest warden. In 1938 he told two schoolboys to plant dozens of larches in a particular pattern, paying them 9 pfennigs per tree. On the ground, you won't notice anything, but flying over Zernikow in late autumn, you suddenly discover the swastika. While the original pine trees stay green in winter, the larches planted by the forest warden turn brown, forming a 60 by 60 m swastika. It was discovered in 1992 on an aerial photograph, and when the local newspaper reported the find, journalists flocked to the site, including even some from the French newspaper „Le Figaro". Repeated attempts to remove the swastika by chopping the trees failed. The „brown seed" (German metaphor for the Nazi ideology) keeps coming through. More tree clearing is to follow, and it is hoped that over the years the swastika will disappear. The best trees are to remain, though, until they have reached the age of 150 years, when the wood will fetch the best price.

48
Brandenburg-Görden Penitentiary

⌂ 1935 → Anton-Saefkow-Allee 2, Brandenburg/Havel, Map A4 The penitentiary was built in 1935. Up to 4800 prisoners were detained here, among them Erich Honecker, the later party leader and head of state of the GDR, sentenced to ten year's hard labor by the ▷„People's Court" in 1937. Also imprisoned here since 1943 was Robert Havemann, later the figurehead of East-German opposition. Thousands of prisoners from many countries in Europe suffered under the inhuman conditions. By 1945, 1722 political prisoners had been executed, 652 died of diseases or malnutrition. After the penitentiary was liberated by the Red Army on 27 April 1945, it was used by the Soviet military to detain war criminals or collaborators. In 1949, the GDR judicial authorities took over the prison and locked up dissidents for years. At the former execution site a small documentation center has been set up. The guillotine now belongs to the German Historical Museum (Deutsches Historisches Museum) in Berlin (to be opened in 2006).

The „Swastika Forest"

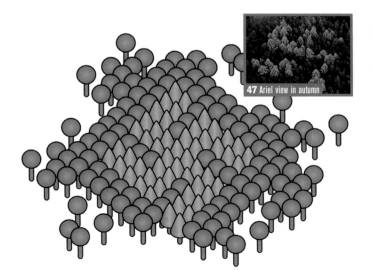

47 Ariel view in autumn

Glossary

Einsatzgruppe – task force squad; SS murder squads in the Eastern occupied territories

Flak (Flugabwehrkanone) – anti-aircraft artillery

Gauleiter – high-ranking Nazi official, appointed by Hitler and responsible for a particular region in Germany; later also in Austria and Czechoslovakia

Gestapo (Geheime Staatspolizei) – Secret State Police

KZ (Konzentrationslager) – concentration camp

Leibstandarte SS – SS unit specifically charged with the protection of the „Führer"

Nazi – abbreviation for National Socialists

NSDAP (National Socialist German Workers Party) – official name of the Nazi party

Nürnberg (also spelt **Nuremberg** in English) – location for huge Nazi party rallies; later seat of the international military tribunal against German war criminals

OKW (Oberkommando der Wehrmacht) – Armed Forces Supreme Command

RSHA (Reichssicherheitshauptamt) – Reich Security Head Office

SA (Sturmabteilung) – storm troops; paramilitary organization of the Nazi party

SD (Sicherheitsdienst) – SS Security Service; party intelligence and security organization

SS (Schutzstaffel) – originally an elite guard, which later, under Himmler, developed into a mass army and political police

Volkssturm (peoples' storm) – Reserve army made up of Hitler Youth, women and elderly men

Wehrmacht – German Armed Forces (Army, Navy, Air force)

Bundeswehr – Armed Forces of the Federal Republic of Germany

DDR (Deutsche Demokratische Republik) – German Democratic Republic; official name for East Germany or GDR

BRD (Bundesrepublik Deutschland) – Federal Republic of Germany; official name for West Germany or FRG

NVA (Nationale Volksarmee) – army of the GDR

Plattenbau – a building made of large, prefabricated concrete slabs, often found in central and eastern Europe. The word is a compound of Platte (slab) and Bau (building)

SED (Sozialistische Einheitspartei) – Socialist Unity Party; Communist party of the GDR

Select Bibliography

Arnold, Dietmar; Janick, Reiner: Sirenen und gepackte Koffer. Bunkeralltag in Berlin, Berlin 2003.

Balfour, Alan: Berlin – The Politics of Order 1737–1989. New York 1990

Beevor, Antony: The Fall of Berlin 1945. New York 2003

Benz, Wolfgang; Graml, Hermann; Weiß, Hermann: Enzyklopädie des Nationalsozialismus, München 1998.

Chod, Katrin; Schwenk, Herbert; Weisspflug, Hainer: Berlin Mitte. Das Lexikon, Berlin 2001.

Demps, Laurenz: Berlin Wilhelmstraße. Eine Topographie preußisch-deutscher Macht, Berlin 2000.

Enke, Roland: Berlin: Offene Stadt. Die Stadt als Ausstellung. Der Wegweiser, Berlin 2000.

Fest, Joachim C.: Speer. Eine Biografie, Berlin 1999.

Fest, Joachim C.: Der Untergang. Hitler und das Ende des Dritten Reiches. Eine historische Skizze, Berlin 2002.

Kästner, Erich: Notabene 45. Ein Tagebuch, München 1983.

Knopf, Volker; Martens, Stefan: Görings Reich. Selbstinszenierung in Carinhall, Berlin 1999.

Reichhardt, Hans J.; Schäche, Wolfgang: Von Berlin nach „Germania". Über die Zerstörung der „Reichshauptstadt" durch Albert Speers Neugestaltungsplanungen, Berlin 1998.

Schäche, Wolfgang: Architektur und Städtebau in Berlin zwischen 1933 und 1945. Planen und Bauen unter der Ägide der Stadtverwaltung, Berlin 1992.

Schulte-Peevers, Andrea and Tom Parkinson: Berlin City Guide. Lonely Planet 2004

Snyder, Louis L.: Encyclopedia of the Third Reich. London 1998

Speer, Albert: Inside the Third Reich. New York 1970

Spotts, Frederic; Hitler and the Power of Aesthetics. New York 2003

Taylor, Ronald: Berlin and its Culture: A Historical Portrait. New Haven 1997

Imprint

A catalogue record for this publication is available from the Deutsche Bibliothek in the Deutsche Nationalbibliographie; detailed bibliographical data are available on the internet at
http://dnb.ddb.de
First edition, June 2005
© Christoph Links Verlag
LinksDruck GmbH, 2005
Schönhauser Allee 36
10435 Berlin
Tel.: +49 30 44 02 32-0
www.linksverlag.de
mail@linksverlag.de

Front cover design: Maik Kopleck

Text/Design/Illustrations:
Maik Kopleck, STAAB/KOPLECK:DESIGN!
www.staab-kopleck-design.de

DTP: Marina Siegemund, Berlin

Printed by: Bosch-Druck GmbH, Landshut

ISBN 3-86153-363-4

Maik Kopleck

Born in 1975, studied Communication Design at the University of Applied Sciences in Düsseldorf, was free-lance Art Director with several advertising agencies in Düsseldorf and Berlin. Then free-lance photographer in San Francisco; co-director of the design company STAAB/KOPLECK:DESIGN! in Düsseldorf, founded in 1996.

Acknowledgements

Special thanks to Hans Kopleck, Brigitte Staab, Ernst Staab, Prof. Werner Holzwarth, Morris Aberham, Dr. Robert Kuhn, Prof. Vilibald Barl, Lena Brombacher, Alexander Römer, Martin Venn, Susanne Büker and Jens Kamphausen.

Photographs

On pages with several photos or illustrations, the source is given beginning from the top to the bottom of the page and from left to right. All photos, maps and illustrations without acknowledgement are from the author or the publisher. In a few cases the rightful copyright owners could not be identified.

Alliierten-Museum, Berlin/Atlanta-Service Frankfurt a.M.: p. 72/73

Archiv Dietmar Arnold, Verein Berliner Unterwelten: p. 15 l., 41

Archiv Lena Brombacher: p. 7 l., 7 r., 23 bottom middle r., 24 bottom r., 60 bottom middle, 60 bottom middle l., 60 bottom r.

Archiv Michael Foedrowitz: p. 41 bottom r., 68 middle l., 74 top, 74 top r., 82 bottom middle r.

Archiv Reiner Janick, Verein Berliner Unterwelten: p. 15 middle, 40, 42 top.

Bildarchiv Preußischer Kulturbesitz: p. 6, 10 top left (both), 10 bottom l., 17 bottom., 37 middle bottom r., 44, 45 bottom r., 52 top., 64 bottom l., 68 l., 82 bottom.

Bundesarchiv Koblenz: p. 2, 78 l.

Deutsches Historisches Museum Berlin: p. 17 bottom r., 52 bottom, 84 top.

Fotobestand W. Schäche, Berlin: p. 29, 32 (both), 37 top l., 37 top r., 37 bottom middle r., 37 bottom middle l., 37 bottom l., 38/39

Gedenkstätte Deutscher Widerstand, Berlin: p. 20 top l.

Getty-Images: p. 46

Landesarchiv Berlin: p. 8 middle, 10 top r., 48

Marco-VG: p. 11

Thomas Kemnitz; Berlin, vimudeap.de: p. 77 top r.

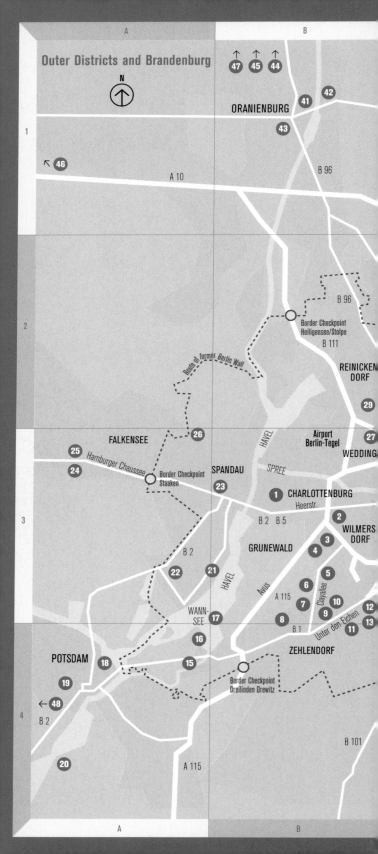

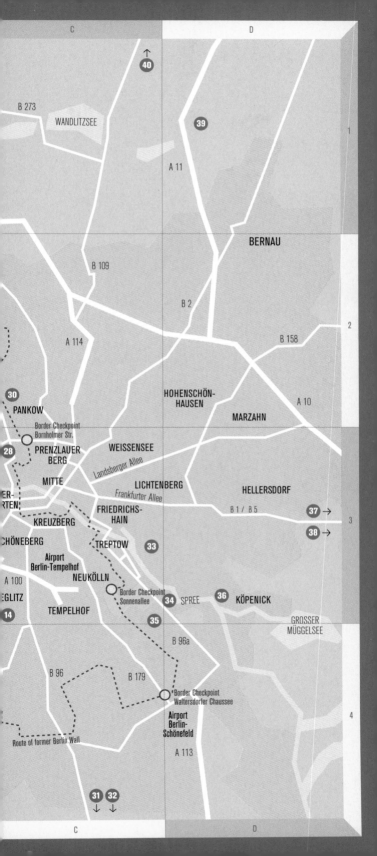